LANDMARKS IN THE HISTORY
OF EARLY CHRISTIANITY

THE MACMILLAN COMPANY
NEW YORK · BOSTON · CHICAGO · DALLAS
ATLANTA · SAN FRANCISCO

MACMILLAN & CO., LIMITED
LONDON · BOMBAY · CALCUTTA
MELBOURNE

THE MACMILLAN CO. OF CANADA, LTD.
TORONTO

LANDMARKS IN THE HISTORY
OF
EARLY CHRISTIANITY

BY

KIRSOPP LAKE, D.D.

New York

THE MACMILLAN COMPANY

1922

Press of
J. J. Little & Ives Company
New York, U. S. A.

TO
H. R.

PREFACE

THE following chapters are the lectures given in the spring of 1919 on the Haskell Foundation of Oberlin College. They have been somewhat expanded in the course of preparation for the press, but have not been materially changed.

At the time of the delivery of these lectures I was busy with the chapter on "Primitive Christianity" in the *Prolegomena to Acts,* and was glad of the opportunity to re-state some of the conclusions reached in that book in a less technical form and with more attention to their bearing on some of the larger questions of religion and thought, such as the Teaching of Jesus, the Hope of Immortality, and the Development of Christology. I did not hesitate to make use of one or two paragraphs from the larger book, and I think that my friend, Mr. C. G. Montefiore, will forgive me for having borrowed two beautiful stories from his chapter in it.

I am greatly indebted to the Faculty of Oberlin College not only for the privilege of lecturing to them, but also for the hospitality extended to me during a very pleasant week and for the beginning of new and delightful friendships.

KIRSOPP LAKE.

CAMBRIDGE, MASS.,
April, 1920.

CONTENTS

CHAPTER I

GALILEE

CHAPTER V

Rome and Ephesus

APPENDIX

LANDMARKS IN THE HISTORY
OF EARLY CHRISTIANITY

LANDMARKS IN THE EARLY HISTORY OF CHRISTIANITY

I

GALILEE

AT first sight the historian of religions appears to be faced by a number of clearly distinguished entities, to each of which he feels justified in giving the name of a separate religion; but on further consideration it becomes obvious that each one of these entities has been in a condition of flux throughout its history. Each began as a combination or synthesis of older forms of thought with comparatively little new in its composition; each ended by disintegrating into many elements, of which the worst disappeared, while the best were taken up into new life in some new religion. The movement was more marked at some times than at others, and the differentiation of the various religions depends chiefly on the recognition of these moments of more rapid change. But the process never really stopped; from beginning to end new elements were constantly absorbed and old elements dropped. For religion lives through the death of religions.

Nothing illustrates this so well as the history of Christianity, for no religion is so well known. The facts are plainly visible, and would be plainly seen by all, were it not for the general tendency of ecclesiastical scholarship to consult the records of the past only to find the reflection of its own features.

The general condition of religion in the Roman Empire at the beginning of the Christian era was one of far advanced disintegration and rapid synthesis. In every district there could be found the remains of old local religions, which retained the loyalty of the conservative, but no longer aroused any vital response in the emotions of the multitudes or in the interest of the educated. At that time, and for many generations afterward, the Roman landowners, to take one example, maintained the ceremonies and customs of an agricultural animism which for their ancestors had been a living religion, but for them had become aesthetic, conventional, and superstitious,— an appendage to life, not its driving force. Those who wish can read a description of it, written with a sympathy possible only for one who felt the analogy of his own experience, in the pages of *Marius the Epicurean,* in which Walter Pater, by a wonderful *tour de force,* wove an exact and scholarly knowledge of the original documents into such a web of artistic English that the deep learning of the book cannot be appreciated except by those who have some small share in it themselves.

Over these local religions had been thrown throughout the Empire the covering fabric of Greek mythology. It had lost much of its power; it was no longer sincerely believed; it was in every respect decadent; but it still played its part in unifying, and to some extent civilising, the diverse races of the Empire. But more important than the Greek mythology was the Greek philosophy, which was indeed in many ways its antidote. If the mythology of Greece appeared to sanction an infinite number of gods and goddesses, her philosophers taught with equal persuasiveness that the divine reality is one, though its forms be many. A remarkable synthesis was thus gradually accomplished, though it will always be a question whether the stronger tendency was to philosophise mythology or to mythologise philosophy.

Yet another element was provided by the stream of

Oriental religions which were coming into the Empire.
Though these religions had all of them at one time been
national, quite as much as the religion of Greece or Rome,
their adherents had been detached violently by the con-
quering hand of Rome from adherence to ancestral shrines
or to political institutions. The Cappadocian or the
Syrian, or even the Egyptian, who was travelling as a
merchant or living as a slave in the western parts of the
Empire, brought with him the worship of his own god;
but the changed conditions of his life were reflected in
his religion. As a political entity his country had disappeared; the institutions which were originally bound up
with the name of his god had vanished, and had become
an ever-fading memory. What these men without coun-
tries asked for was personal salvation, and this they believed that they could find in their mysterious worship.
Each of these religions was rapidly developing in the
first century into a sacramental cult which offered the
blessing of partial protection in this world, and of a happy
immortality after death to all who accepted and were
accepted by its divine lord, and took part in its sacraments or mysteries.

Much is obscure in their history, even though hypothesis
be given the widest range and a friendly hearing. The
central problem, which still requires much further attention than it has as yet received, is how and when these
religions became mystery cults. As we know them in
the Roman Empire all have the same central feature of
offering personal salvation to their adherents through
sacraments. But did they have this characteristic in their
original homes, where they were national religions? The
evidence that they did so is not convincing, and perhaps
cannot be, because of the absence of literary sources. For
instance, one of the best known of these religions is the
cult of Isis, for the nature of which in the second and
third centuries there is admirable evidence in the writings
of Plutarch and Apuleius. It was then clearly a sacra-

mental religion offering private salvation. It was also connected with a myth which was obviously a hindrance rather than a help to these educated Romans, and this myth can be traced back to the monuments of ancient Egypt. Are we justified in concluding that the interpretation in ancient Egypt was the same as in imperial Rome? It may be so; but it is possible that the sacramental nature, though not the element of private salvation came in, in Hellenistic or in Imperial times, to meet the necessity of Egyptians who had lost all sense of belonging to a living nation or having a national religion, and of Greeks who with decadent enthusiasm desired imported rites. In any case, a synthesis was rapidly established between these cults and the official Graeco-Roman religion. The names of the Oriental deities were Hellenised, and the barbaric crudities of the East were removed by allegory and symbolism; the philosophers felt that the myths only needed restatement to confirm their opinions, while the priests were confident that the elements of truth in philosophy were those revealed by the language and ritual of the cults.[1]

With considerable rapidity, therefore, Greek mythology, Greek philosophy, and Oriental cults were being accommodated to one another, and brought together in a new and highly complex religious system. For political purposes the introduction into this system of the worship of the emperors, living or dead, was of great importance. It tended to unify the whole mass, and the imperial authorities adopted the position, with some reservations, that, provided a man accepted the cult of Caesar and Rome, he could in addition be a member of any other religion which pleased his fancy or soothed his soul.

There was one exception to the ease with which the

[1] The best example of this method of "restatement" is probably Plutarch's *De Iside et Osiride*, which discusses the Egyptian myth and the various explanations given of it in accommodation to philosophic truth. Heathenism did not long survive this kind of help; nor is it surprising that it did not.

Oriental cults accepted the situation. Still inspired by
the instinct which nine hundred years before had made
their prophets fight against syncretism, the Jews reso-
lutely refused to come to terms with heathen religions.
Some, indeed, accepted the Greek philosophy, as the writings of Philo and the Wisdom Literature show; but with
the cults or with the mythology of the heathen no compro-
mise was tolerated.

It would be interesting to know how far the imperial
leaders perceived the process of synthesis, but consciously
or unconsciously they helped it considerably by the policy
which they adopted towards the local councils, or Synedria
—Sanhedrims—as they were often called.[1] They were
willing to encourage their continuance, allowing them to
control all local questions of religion, and indeed all local
interests generally, on condition that they made themselves also responsible for the cult of Rome and of Caesar.
In this way Caesar was introduced into the local religion,
and, what was much more important, the local religion
was absorbed into the unified system of the Empire. The
policy was almost uniformly successful: the one exception
was the Sanhedrim of the Jews, which obstinately refused
the imperial cult and resisted Caligula's effort to intro-
duce his statue with the same successful pertinacity as
had repelled the efforts of Antiochus Epiphanes in the
days of the Maccabees. The episode ended disastrously,
for the spirit of nationalism and unreasoning hate to the
government of Rome roused a rebellion which inevitably
led to the fall of Jerusalem and the violent destruction of
Jewish national life. Henceforward the official Jewish
religion remained a foreign element in the life of the
western world. It could not die, for in spite of rabbinical
extravagances it possessed more ethical truth than heathenism, and was more sincere in its protest against supersti-
tion. But neither could it form a synthesis with the
better elements of the Roman world; the process of accom-

[1] See *Prolegomena to Acts,* i. 199-216.

modation to Greek philosophy was stopped for many centuries, and the Jew had neither part nor lot in the life of the empire in which necessity compelled him to live.

Nevertheless in the end the inevitable synthesis between Judaism and Greek thought was accomplished, though the official world was unable to bring it about. The small and at first despised sect of Christians was driven out of the Synagogue and forced into contact with the heathen world, at first probably against its will. There is nothing to show that Christians originally desired to break away from Judaism or to approach the Greeks; yet they did both. When their fellow-countrymen refused to hear they turned to the Gentiles, and there ensued rapidly the abandonment of Jewish practice and the assimilation of Greek and Graeco-Oriental thought.

From that time on the history of Christianity might be written as a series of syntheses with the thought and practice of the Roman world, beginning with the circumference and moving to the centre. The first element which was absorbed was the least Roman, the Graeco-Oriental cults. Christianity had been originally the worship of God, as he was understood by the Jews, combined with the belief that Jesus was he whom God had appointed, or would appoint, as his representative at the day of judgement. To this were now joined the longings for private salvation of the less fortunate classes in the Roman Empire, and their belief that this salvation could come from sacraments instituted by a Lord who was either divine by nature or had attained apotheosis. It thus became, partly indeed, the recognition of the Jewish God as supreme, but chiefly the recognition of Jesus as the divine Lord who had instituted saving mysteries for those who accepted him. Christianity became the Jewish contribution to the Oriental cults, offering, as the Synagogue never did, private salvation by supernatural means to all who were willing to accept it.

Such Christianity became, and such in some districts,

notably in Rome, it remained for one or two generations.
But in Ephesus and possibly elsewhere a further synthesis
was accomplished. This sacramentalised Christianity began to come to terms with Greek philosophy, as the other
mystery religions tried to do. It asked what was the
philosophic explanation of its Lord, and it hit on the
device of identifying him with the Logos—a phrase common to several types of philosophy though used in quite
different meanings.

The development of this second synthesis was comparatively slow. Probably some of the systems which are
loosely described as gnostic were unsuccessful attempts at
its accomplishment; but in the end the Alexandrian theologians Clement and Origen followed the lead given them
by the Fourth Gospel and some of the apologists to the
triumphant construction of a system which really reconciled in part and seemed to reconcile entirely the Christian cult and the later Platonic metaphysics.

Although the general fabric of the Christian philosophy
which was thus built up was in the main Platonic, not a
little was borrowed also from the system of the Stoics, especially on the border ground between metaphysics and
ethics. This paved the way for a further synthesis, accomplished more easily, more thoroughly, and with less
perceptible controversy than had attended either of the
others.

Probably the culmination of this conquest of the
Christian Church by the ethics of the Stoa was reached by
Ambrose, who gave to the Christian world Cicero's popu-
larisation of Panaetius and Posidonius in a series of ser-
mons which extracted the ethics of Rome from the scriptures of the Christians. The ethics of the Stoics were
almost wholly adopted by the leaders of Christian thought,
especially in the West, and the teaching of Jesus as represented in the Gospels was interpreted in the interests
of this achievement, which, like the other syntheses, was
largely effective in proportion as it was unconscious.

Probably it was the early stages of this movement which
had rendered possible the acceptance by one another of
Christianity and the Empire. Certainly there is still
much need of study, even if it produce only the statement
of problems, as to the changed character of Christianity
between the time of Tertullian and Eusebius.

The next few centuries, so far as they were not occupied
in struggling against the eclipse of civilisation which began
in the fifth century, were occupied in working out the
implications of these syntheses. The results were codified
in Catholic theology and in the civil and canon law of the
early Middle Ages. But one more step remained; after
nearly a thousand years Aristotle was rediscovered, and
the final achievement of Christian theology was the synthesis effected by St. Thomas Aquinas between the Christian theology and the philosophy of Aristotle.

It is a great record of great achievement, for no one
who studies the history of religions with any degree of
sympathetic insight can doubt but that each synthesis
was a real step in progress towards that unification of
aspiration with knowledge which it is the task of theologians to bring about, and to express as clearly as
they may.

Many centuries have passed since the time of St.
Thomas Aquinas, and the element of tragedy in the study
of the history of religions for the Christian theologian
is that he is forced to admit that never again has there
been a time when the unification of aspiration and knowledge has been so completely realised by organised Christianity. It was not long after this time that epoch-making
changes were made, first in the domain of astronomy and
afterwards in other sciences. They have revolutionised
human knowledge. Nor have human aspirations stayed
where they were. The ideal of justice which men see
to-day is different and assuredly better than that of a
thousand years ago. It extends beyond the sphere of the
law-courts to every branch of human life. But the doc-

trines of the Church remain formulated according to the
knowledge and aspirations of the past. The divergence
between knowledge and theological statement has become
more and more obvious every year. There has been no
synthetic progress in theology since the time of St. Thomas
Aquinas,[1] for it is impossible for the student of history
to feel that the Reformation can be regarded as a synthesis. Indeed it seems ominously like the first step in
that disintegration which has always been the last stage
in the story of each religion. It is absolutely certain that
the world will once again some day achieve what it has
often had and often lost—the closer approximation of
knowledge and aspiration—so that its religious system
may satisfy the soul of the saint without disgusting the
intellect of the scholar. What is uncertain is whether
this achievement will be made by any form of organised
Christianity or is reserved for some movement which cannot at present be recognised.[2]

To trace the whole of these syntheses would be a rea-
sonable programme for many volumes. These lectures are
limited to the discussion of the evolution of the first and
the beginning of the second—that is to say, the change of
Christianity from a Jewish sect to a sacramental cult and
the beginning of the movement which introduced Greek
metaphysics into its theology.

At the beginning of the first century the control of the
Jewish nation was in the hands partly of Rome, partly of
the high-priests and their families. The latter, as was
natural, held in the main a conservative attitude towards
the laws and customs of their people. They were rich
men—some of them probably could appreciate the culture

[1] Ritschlianism is perhaps an exception: it did at least attempt a
synthesis with science approached through Kantian philosophy. But
was it successful?

[2] No one has seen this more clearly, or expressed it more vividly,
than the late George Tyrrell, especially in his *A Much Abused Letter*
and *Christianity at the Cross-roads.*

if not the thought of Rome—and the class in modern
Europe which most closely resembles them is that of the
aristocratic Turks of Constantinople—orthodox but not
enthusiastic adherents of the religion of their fathers.
They doubtless regarded themselves as the leaders of the
people: it was with them, naturally enough, that the
Roman world had to deal, and the price of their failure
to keep the peace between the populace and Rome was
their political extinction and their personal ruin.   The
populace demanded that the leaders should secure national
independence; Rome required that they should induce
the people to cease from asking it.   The task was an impossible one, but history does not accept impossibility as
an excuse for failure.

Closely connected with them were the Herods, who at
intervals assumed a more or less dominating influence in
Jewish affairs.   At the time of Christ one of the family
was ruling over Galilee, and another was destined in a
short time to inherit not only this dominion but also that
of Judaea.   But though for political purposes the Herods
were capable of playing Jewish cards, they had become
completely absorbed into the cosmopolitan society of the
Empire.   They were as little typical of anything really
Jewish as an educated Indian prince frequenting London
society is typical of Hinduism.

Ultimately more important than the high-priests or the
Herods were two other classes which were destined respectively to ruin their nation and to save their church.
The one was the party of the patriots, the other the Scribes
and Pharisees.

After the death of Herod the Great the Romans made a
census of his country, and a certain Judas of Galilee endeavoured to raise an active rebellion.   The influence of
the ruling classes in Jerusalem suppressed this movement
for the time, but it remained, as Josephus [1] terms it, the

---

[1] Josephus, *Antiq.* xviii. 1. 1 and 6.   See also *Prolegomena to Acts*,
i. 421 ff.

fourth philosophy, or sect, among the Jews, maintaining that no pious Jew could recognise any ruler except God, and steadily insisting that active resistance to the power of Rome was justifiable and even necessary. The sect apparently remained anonymous until about A.D. 66, when one branch of those who accepted its tenets took to themselves the name of Zealots and were largely instrumental in bringing about those final disturbances which led to the fall of Jerusalem. We know very little of this party except from Josephus, and the reasons for which his book was written did not encourage him to give unnecessary information, but, judging by results, the fourth philosophy must have been in the first half of the first century a steadily growing menace to all organised government, willing to destroy but unable to build, concealing under the name of patriotism that pathological excitement which is the delirium of diseased nations.

It is possible, but not certain, that these Jews were influenced by and possibly helped to produce some parts of that curious literature known as Apocalypses,[1] which seems in the main to have been intended to comfort the discouraged and to inspire them with enthusiasm by giving them the assurance that a better time was at hand.

A very different type of Jew was represented by the Scribes and Pharisees. They believed implicitly that the law of Moses and the tradition of the elders had a divine sanction, and that to live in accordance with it, not to take part in political intrigue, was the way of Life. Their main object was to interpret the Law in such a way as to make it possible to follow, and to extend its explanation so as to cover every possible problem in practical life. They were opposed to Jesus during his life, and afterwards bitterly opposed to his followers. It is therefore

---

[1] This literature is now available as a whole in R. H. Charles, *Apocrypha and Pseudepigrapha.*

natural that there is in the Christian Scriptures a large amount of polemic against the Pharisees,[1] and there would be probably more against the Christians in the rabbinical writings had it not been for the activities of the mediaeval censors, so that statements in the Talmud which originally referred to the Christians are concealed (sometimes obviously but in other cases probably successfully) by being referred to the Sadducees or other extinct parties of Jews for whose reputation neither Synagogue nor Church cared.

Owing to the fact that generations of Christians have seen the early history of the Scribes and Pharisees almost wholly through glasses coloured by early controversy, it is hard to be fair to the Pharisees. Taken at their best they probably represent the highest form of a religion based on codified ethics which the world has ever seen. They did not feel that the Law was external, for it represented the will of the Father, which could not be alien to that of his children if they understood it aright. The "word" was not in heaven or across the sea, but very nigh unto them, in their mouth and in their heart that they might do it. That is to say, the Law was not something imposed entirely from without by a wholly external authority, but was rather the very perfect expression of what man would of himself choose to do if he had perfect knowledge. Thus the best of the Pharisees no doubt felt that obedience to the Law and to tradition was a labour of love, and the story which is told of the death of Akiba may be regarded as typical of the best both of his predecessors and successors. He was being put to death by torture when the hour came that every pious Jew repeats the

[1] The suggestion has even been made that some of the polemic in the gospels, which is—as the text stands—directed against the Pharisees and Rabbis, was historically intended for the Sadducees. It was too important to be lost, and, as those who were originally attacked had ceased to be important, it was turned against the only Jewish party which still survived to oppose Christianity at the time when the gospels were written. See also p. 24.

Shema, "Thou shalt love the Lord thy God with all thy heart and with all thy soul." He recited as far as "with all thy heart," and then stopped and smiled. "How," said one of the bystanders, "can you smile when you are dying in agony?" "Every day," he replied, "have I repeated these words, and I could say without hesitation that I loved the Lord with all my heart, but to say that I loved him with all my soul, that is to say, with all my life, was hard, for how can a man say what he has done with his life before the day of his death? But now that the day of my death has come and the hour for repeating the Shema has returned, and I have loved the Lord my God with all my heart and with all my life, why should I not smile?" [1]

It is not surprising that it was the school of these men who saved the Jewish Church from extinction when the nation was destroyed; neither is it surprising, though it is sad, that there was deep hatred between them and the Christians; for in religion, as in other things, a really lively hatred requires some degree of relationship.

It was into this world of Jewish thought and practice that Jesus came preaching in Galilee. The content of his preaching is given by Mark as "Repent, for the Kingdom of Heaven is at hand." Therefore the two questions of primary importance are the meaning of the Kingdom of Heaven or Kingdom of God, and of repentance.

The phrase "the Kingdom of Heaven" is common in the later Jewish literature and familiar in Christian ears. But it is not actually found before the Christian era, though similar expressions were customary, and the concept which it covers is often met with in the Old Testament. It means primarily the sovereignty of God in the

---

[1] This is a free rendering, somewhat paraphrased to bring out the meaning, of the account of the martyrdom of Akiba under Tinnius (Turnus) Rufus in the Jerusalem Talmud (*Berakh.* ix. 7). See *Prolegomena to Acts*, I. 62.

world, not a kingdom in the local sense, or even in the sense of an organisation. Though in the Old Testament God is frequently referred to as a king whose rule is universal even now, the dominion of a king is not complete or perfect unless he be recognised by his subjects, and the dominion of God is not yet thus recognised or submitted to throughout the world. The Jewish view seems to have been that men had fallen away from the rule of God in the days before Abraham, and that when Abraham recognised the Lord as his God, then for him—but not for others—the sovereignty of God was complete. Similarly, when Israel recognised the Lord as their God there was a nation which accepted the sovereignty of God. The time would come when all the world would make this same recognition, but the day was not yet present, and there was more than one opinion as to the probable course of events which would lead up to it.

In general the Jews believed that the universal recognition of the sovereignty of God would bring about, or would at least be coincident with, the coming of the Golden Age, so frequently spoken of by the prophets, and described with imaginative profusion in the apocalyptic writings. But it is by no means always clear whether the Golden Age was the condition or the result of the coming of the Kingdom. Would the heathen, who knew not God, be converted or be exterminated? It is not surprising if there was a tendency to confuse the recognition of the sovereignty of God with the phenomena attending it, and to speak of the Kingdom of God when the conditions of its attainment were really meant.

There were two special features in the Jewish expectation of the future recognition of the sovereignty of God which were especially liable to be confused with it in this manner. In the first place, some of the prophets had spoken of the coming of the Golden Age and the restoration of the national fortunes of Israel. Sometimes this restoration had been associated with the house of David, sometimes with the dynasty of the high priest; but frequently no such association was present, and Christian scholarship has in general greatly exaggerated the amount of evidence, especially for a Davidic king. The reason for this exaggeration is partly verbal. The custom has arisen of speaking of this Golden Age as the "Messianic" Age, which can only mean the age in which the "Messiah" will appear. "Messiah" is itself a technical term, but "Messianic" can only be applied to a person appointed by God to some high office, and to a period of history only if such a person be central in it. The really most striking feature of most of the descriptions of the Golden Age in the Old Testament and in the apocalyptic books is that there is no mention of any Messiah at all. But the later literature emphasised the coming of King Messiah, and the Jews therefore refer to this period as "the days of the Messiah." There is no evidence that this phrase was used until after the Christian era. For this reason it is a great pity that scholars, who personally, of course, know better, constantly use so misleading a term as the Messianic Age. It would be far better if it were described as the "Golden Age" or the "good time." [1]

This whole conception of the coming Golden Age was in essence peculiarly Jewish, though parallels can be found in the religion of all nations. Cognate to it was another point of view which was not originally Jewish, but had probably been taken over by the Jews from Persian thought. This was the expectation of the Age to Come, which plays so large a part in the fourth book of Ezra [2]

[1] J. Klausner's *Die messianische Vorstellungen des jüdischen Volkes im Zeitalter der Tannaiten* is probably the clearest statement of the facts.

[2] The fourth book of Ezra is in many ways the finest of all Apocalypses, and the English authorised version (in which it is called 2 Esdras) is a magnificent piece of English, needing, however, occasional elucidation and correction by the critical editions of G. H. Box, *The Ezra Apocalypse*, and of B. Violet, in the edition of the Greek Christian writers of the first three centuries published by the Berlin Academy.

and in the later literature. An integral part of the Persian system was the belief that the world would come
to an end and be consumed by fire which would purify
it from evil, after which the righteous would be raised
from the dead and take part in the glorious life of a new
world. A supernatural figure known as the Shaoshyant
would take part in this process, and especially in the
Judgement which would decide whether men should or
should not pass on into the life of the Age to Come.

From the time of Daniel, if not earlier, these ideas had
been absorbed by the Jews, and though belief in a resurrection was not universal it had been accepted by the
Pharisees, and was probably more popular than either
the ancient Jewish belief in Sheol or the imported Greek
belief in the immortality of the soul, of which traces can
be found in the Wisdom Literature. All this is, however,
different from the ancient Jewish tradition of a Golden
Age in this world, and there are plain traces in Jewish
literature of the attempt to reconcile the two systems.

It was obviously possible, by dint of a comparatively
small confusion of thought, to identify the Golden Age
with the Age to Come, and to suppose that all the unful-
filled features of the visions of the earlier prophets would
be realised in the Age to Come. In this case the figure
of the Davidic king, if he happened to be part of the picture, could easily be transplanted into the Age to Come,
and whereas in the earlier presentation he had the special
function of destroying in a holy war the enemies of Israel,
he could now have the more universal responsibility of
abolishing all evil, and of acting as judge to decide who
should enter into the new world.

It is on general principles entirely probable that some
such accommodation of thought was effected in some
Jewish circles, as it was afterwards among the Christians.
But there is comparatively little evidence that such was
actually the case. Especially is there very little evidence
that the anointed Son of David was transmuted in this

fashion. The most that can be said is that some of the many titles which were applied to the expected Davidic king were also applied to the expected supernatural judge. But identity of title does not always mean identity of person, and the general descriptions of the two figures are as a rule quite separate. It would appear that on the whole the better Jews in the time of Christ were looking for the End of the Age and the Resurrection, rather than for the restoration of the kingdom of David, but that there was a popular minority which still had hopes of the restoration of the monarchy.

The most thorough attempt to reconcile the two lines of thought is to be found in the fourth book of Ezra, which elaborates a complete combination of both systems with a clearness quite unusual in apocalyptic literature. According to this the time was approaching when the Messiah, by which is clearly meant the king of Israel, would appear, destroy all opposition, and reign for four hundred years. He and all mankind would then die. The world would come to an end and be restored to primaeval silence. Then would follow the Resurrection and Judgement, and the beginning of the Age to Come. All the features of both systems are thus combined, except that it appears that the Judgement is the act of God himself, rather than of an especially appointed representative.

The general result of reading the literature belonging to this period is to create the impression that recent scholarship has gone much further than is justifiable in the attempt to systematise Jewish thought on eschatology. It has succumbed too readily to the temptation to find system where there is none, to base a chronological development of thought on the discovery, and finally to emend the texts in its light, and sometimes in its aid. It seems extremely doubtful whether there was any "generally recognised" Jewish teaching on this subject. The belief that God would deliver his people, and that his sovereignty would be recognised throughout the world, was no doubt part of the belief of every pious Jew, but the details were vague and there was no systematic teaching on them.

If we turn to the gospels we find that the Kingdom of God is sometimes looked for in the future, sometimes regarded as a present reality. Scholarship in the last fifteen years has passed through a period in which the presence of these two elements has been somewhat hotly debated. The beginning of the discussion was probably the publication of Johannes Weiss' monograph [1] on the preaching of Jesus as to the Kingdom of God, in which he emphasised the future aspect of the Kingdom. The question was, however, presented with greater perspective as to its position in the history of criticism by A. Schweitzer in a book which he called *Von Reimarus zu Wrede*. This was translated into English,[2] a fate denied to Weiss, with the result that in England and America the whole problem was associated with Schweitzer's name. The position adopted by these writers was that the teaching of Jesus was mainly eschatological, that is to say, it looked forward to the coming of the end of the world. In the enthusiasm of the rediscovery of this point of view—by no means unknown to our ancestors, and universal in the early Church —Schweitzer and others went rather further than the evidence permitted, and endeavoured to explain eschatologically passages not susceptible of that meaning, but that does not excuse the foolish acrimony with which the less learned, especially among liberal Protestants, assailed them, nor the attempt to cut out from the text of the gospels all eschatological reference.

At present the question has apparently reached equilibrium by the general recognition that it is impossible to excise or to explain away the passages in the gospels in which the Kingdom of Heaven is clearly regarded as future, and that it is equally impossible to ignore those

---

[1] J. Weiss, *Die Predigt Jesu vom Reiche Gottes*. The first edition of this book is smaller and better than the second.
[2] The *Quest of the Historic Jesus*.

in which it is regarded as a present reality. Probably,
however, it has even now not been sufficiently perceived
that the solution of the problem is not to be found in
the literary criticism of the gospels, but in the history of
the phrase, Kingdom of God. This rendered inevitable
the double use of the phrase. Sometimes it was used
strictly, and referred to a present reality within the grasp
of all willing to reach out to it, and accept the conditions
imposed on its attainment, of which Jesus was so frequently speaking. But at other times, by an entirely
natural extension of its meaning, it was used of the period
when the recognition of the sovereignty of God would be
universal. In this sense it was still future. It was at
hand, but not yet present, even though that generation
would not entirely pass away before it was accomplished.
There is no exegetical obstacle to accepting this view, for
it is the plain and simple meaning of simple phrases; but
there is the theological difficulty that it represents an
expectation on the part of Jesus which was falsified by
history.[1] That generation has passed away, and many
others after it, and the Kingdom of God has not yet come.
Indeed, it is scarcely orthodox any longer to expect it in
the manner in which the gospels represent Jesus to have
foretold its coming.

But even when it is conceded that Jesus in some places
in the gospels did undoubtedly contemplate the coming of
the Kingdom in the future, it remains a problem, which
has as yet attracted too little attention, whether he identified the eschatological phenomena attending its coming
with the reign of the anointed scion of the house of David,
or with the end of this age and the inauguration of the Age
to Come. In general it seems to me far more likely that
he looked for the Age to Come rather than for the reign
of the Son of David, though the evidence is admittedly
not very full or entirely satisfactory. It is, however, at

---

[1] I have endeavoured to deal with this question in the *Stewardship
of Faith,* pp. 36 ff.

least clear that in his answer to the young man who asked Jesus what he should do,[1] eternal life is treated as synonymous with the Kingdom of God. The young man asked what was necessary to inherit eternal life, and when Jesus told him that he should observe the commandments, sell all that he had and give to the poor, he was grieved. Jesus then said, "How hardly will those that have riches enter into the Kingdom of God." Obviously eternal life and the Kingdom of God are here identical, and there is no doubt that the Jews expected eternal life in the Age to Come, not in the Days of the Messiah. Moreover, the continuation of the narrative—the implied question of Peter, "Lo, we have left all and followed thee"—introduces the statement of Jesus, "There is no one who has left home, or brothers, or sisters, or mother, or father, or children, or lands, for my sake and for the good news, who shall not receive a hundredfold now in this time— houses, and brothers, and sisters, and mothers, and children, and lands, with persecutions, and in the Age to Come life everlasting." The distinction here between "this time" and the Age to Come is entirely Jewish, and shows that in the previous paragraph the Kingdom of God and eternal life were associated in the mind of Jesus with the Age to Come.

But, it may be said, did not Jesus identify himself with the Davidic Messiah? Undoubtedly his disciples did so in the circles represented by Matthew and Luke, but it is doubtful whether the gospel of Mark represents this point of view, and the question of Jesus to the Pharisees, how David in the Scriptures could call the Messiah Lord if he were his son, is pointless, except on the assumption that Jesus did not regard himself as the Son of David.[2] On the other hand, the identification of Jesus with the Son of Man, whether by himself or by his disciples, can in no case affect the question, because the figure of the Son of Man in Jewish literature is an integral part of the inau-

[1] Mark x. 17 ff.　　　　　　　　　　　[2] Mark xii. 35.

guration of the Age to Come, not of the reign of the
Davidic king.

Thus it seems probable that one part of the teaching of
Jesus was the announcement that this age is coming to its
end and that the Age to Come is rapidly approaching,
when the Kingdom of God will be universally realised.
Those who wish to pass on into the life of the New Age
must prepare themselves by accepting already the sovereignty of God at whatever cost it may be. Nothing
physicial or social must be allowed to stand in the
way; relations, property, eyesight, hands or feet must
all be sacrificed if they stand between man and his
perfect acceptance of God's sovereignty [1]; few men have
lived up to this standard, and to reach it they must
repent.

Repentance to a Jew in the first century meant primarily change of conduct, but it is a misunderstanding of
the Jewish position to suppose that by this they excluded
or indeed did not definitely intend a change of heart. A
typical example of the meaning of repentance in Jewish
literature is the story of Rabbi Eliezer ben Durdaiya,[2]
who was famous for his consistently immoral life, but was
stung to the heart one day when one of his companions
casually remarked that for him at least no repentance
could avail. Then, continues the story, he went forth,
and sat between the hills, and said, "Ye mountains and
hills, seek mercy for me." But they said, "Before we
seek mercy for you, we must seek it for ourselves, for it
is said, The mountains shall depart and the hills be removed." Then he said, "Heaven and earth, ask mercy
for me." But they said, "Before we ask mercy for you,
we must ask it for ourselves, as it is said, The heavens shall
vanish like smoke, and the earth shall wax old as a gar-
ment." Then he said, "Sun and moon, ask mercy for
me." But they said, "Before we ask for you, we must ask

---

[1] Mark ix. 43 ff.; cf. Matt. v. 29 ff.
[2] Quoted by C. G. Montefiore in the *Prolegomena to Acts,* pp. 71 f.

for ourselves, as it is said, The moon shall be confounded, and the sun ashamed." Then he said, "Planets and stars, ask mercy for me." But they said, "Before we ask for you, we must ask for ourselves, as it is said, All the hosts of heaven shall be dissolved, and the heaven shall be rolled up as a scroll." Then he said, "The matter depends wholly upon me." He sank his head between his knees, and cried and wept so long that his soul went forth from him. Then a heavenly voice was heard to say, "Rabbi Eliezer ben Durdaiya has been appointed to the life of the world to come." But Rabbi Jehudah I., the Patriarch, wept and said, "There are those who acquire the world to come in years upon years; there are those who acquire it in an hour." The story is an admirable parallel to that of the Prodigal Son and shows that the best rabbinical and the best Christian teaching on repentance were identical as to its nature and efficacy.

It is thus clear that there was not any essential difference between Jesus and his contemporaries as to either the meaning of the Kingdom of God or the necessity and power of repentance. The difference between them came in the kind of conduct which was necessary for membership in the Kingdom of God and prescribed for repentance. It was at this point that Jesus came into sharp conflict with the two parties previously described, the Fourth Philosophy and the Scribes and Pharisees.

The difference between Jesus and the Pharisees was one of interpretation. Both he and they regarded the Law as the revelation of God's will, and Jesus himself was emphatic in declaring that it was binding and that he did not wish to destroy it. But the Pharisees endeavoured to make the Law cover every detail of human life by combining it with clever verbal interpretations which stretched its meaning in every direction. Jesus, on the other hand, appealed from the letter of the Law to its original purpose, which he held to be the benefit of

man.[1] If, therefore, there was any contradiction between
the letter of the Law and its original purpose, it was the
purpose which was dominant. No one can doubt that in
this respect Jesus followed a principle incontestably correct but extraordinarily difficult of application. It contains, moreover, implicit in it an appeal to conscience,
for it was really by this rather than by historic knowledge
that the ultimate purpose of the Law was revealed. The
final test of formularies which appeal to the intellect is
whether they are true and of codes defining conduct
whether they are right, but the perception of truth and of
right depends in the end on reason and on conscience,[2]
and the difficulty and obscurity which attend their application constantly frighten men into trying to substitute
some easier way for that of Jesus: but here too the saying
is true that "narrow is the way that leadeth unto life."

Far more deep-seated was the difference between Jesus
and the Fourth Philosophy. It is only necessary to put
oneself back in the position of a Jew of Galilee in the first
century, inspired by the patriotic teaching of Judas of
Galilee and his followers, to understand how extraordinarily unpopular the teaching of Jesus must have been in
Galilee. Such a Jew believed that the continuance of the
Roman rule was an intolerable injustice, that it ought
not to be endured, that resistance to it was right and

[1] See Mark ii. 27. For the meaning of Son of Man in this passage
see p. 38.
[2] Neither reason nor conscience is infallible: the tribunal of history condemns many actions which were undoubtedly dictated by
conscience. Nevertheless we have no better guides in action, and
both reason and conscience have the peculiarity that the more they
are used the better do they become, and conversely that if they be
neglected they cease to be available in time of need. Men who
habitually use their powers in order to circumvent either conscience
or reason in the end find they are unable to use them at all. The
distinction between right and wrong disappears when conscience
dies, and that between fact and fiction when reason is neglected.
The one is the danger which besets clever politicians, the other the
nemesis which waits on popular preachers.

proper and would be crowned with success by the inter-
vention of God. If he heard Jesus say, "Love your
enemies, do good to them that hate you, bless them that
curse you . . . as ye would that men should do to you
do ye to them likewise; for if ye love them that love you
what thank have you . . . love ye your enemies," what
would such a man have thought? In the light of the experiences of our own time there is no reason for wonder
that Jesus in the end found it impossible to live in Galilee.
The marvel is that he escaped with his life.

The contrast between such teaching and that of the
Fourth Philosophy is so obvious that it could never either
escape attention or be denied if it were not for the absence
of any definite mention of this party in the gospels. The
probable explanation is that by the time that the gospels
were written the Fourth Philosophy had ceased to exist,
and that in Greek circles this party was never prominent.
The result was that there was no reason to perpetuate any
tradition as to controversy between Jesus and the Fourth
Philosophy. The only dispute with the Jews in which
the Christians of the generation that produced the gospels
were interested was that with the rabbis, the lineal de-
scendants of the Pharisees. Thus they preserved the story
of arguments between Jesus and the Pharisees, but not
between him and the representatives of other schools.
This, however, did not mean that the teaching of Jesus
called out by the Fourth Philosophy was not preserved.
The teaching itself was given, but, just as in the Talmud
the sayings of rabbis are often given without historic context, so also in Christian tradition the sayings of Jesus
usually appear without the incidents which had called
them out. In exactly the same way, except for the final
scene in Jerusalem, the priests and Sadducees are not
mentioned; they played no part in the life of the Christian
generation which produced the gospels. There was, however, a special reason why the non-resistant teaching of
Jesus should be preserved even when its historic back-

ground was lost. Though the Fourth Philosophy had ceased to have any contact with the Church, the persecution of Christians was an actual problem, and the practical difficulty of right conduct under its stress kept alive teaching which might otherwise have been forgotten.

The question is sometimes asked whether such teaching is really consistent with the violent cleansing of the Temple. The true answer is probably not to be found in any ingenious harmonisation, but rather in accentuating the fact that the "non-resistant" teaching in the Sermon on the Mount deals with the line of conduct to be observed towards foreign oppressors and violence from without. The sacerdotal money-changers and sellers of doves in the Temple were not the "oppressors of Israel." Israel was called on to suffer under Roman rule, and the righteous to endure violence at the hands of the wicked, for that was the will of God, who in his own good time would shorten the evil days. But the manipulation of the sacrificial system as a means of plundering the pious was a sin of Israel itself, against which protest and force were justified. What the heathen and the wicked do is their concern and God's, but the sins of Israel are Israel's own; against them the righteous in Israel may execute judgement.

It would be an affectation to suggest that this subject does not raise questions of the greatest practical importance for the present age; no one is justified in evading the issues presented. The teaching of Jesus represents a non-resistant attitude which has come to be described as "pacifist," and the world has just passed through a crisis which has proved that "pacifism" and "non-resistance" are impossible policies. What does this mean for those who profess and call themselves Christians? It cannot mean that they ought to adopt a non-resistant policy either in personal or in national affairs, for experience (which has, after all, some merit) seems to prove that the policy of not resisting evil leads to its triumph rather than its defeat. But this fact gives no justification for explaining away or watering down the plain and intelligible teaching of Jesus.[1] It was his teaching; it may have been right and wise for his immediate hearers; but it is not wise or right as the general basis of conduct, whether personal or national. If Jesus intended to lay down a general principle of conduct we have to admit that he was wrong, or adopt the pacifist position. There is nothing in the context to suggest that he thought of a limited application of his words, nor in the days of persecution which followed did Christians so interpret him. If, therefore, he was wrong it is necessary to ask how we can explain the error.

The answer seems to lie in a comparison of the attitude adopted by the Jews of the first century on the one hand, and by ourselves on the other, as to the working of God in the world. The Jew believed not merely in an omnipotent God, but in a God who constantly used his power quite independently of the action of men. We, on the contrary, believe that the universe is so constituted that human action bears a fixed relation to the course of events. What men do or do not bears a definite relation to the events which will follow, and we no longer look for God to help those who are unwilling to help themselves. One of the means which we possess of helping ourselves is force, physical force. We have the power to use it for good or for evil. It is as culpable not to use force when occasion requires as it is to use it when occasion does not.

This is tolerably plain to us, but it was not tolerably plain to the Jew of the first century. The war has brought out the human limitations of the ethics of Jesus by the intellectual horizon of his own time as clearly as the application of literary criticism to the Old Testament brought out the defects of his knowledge of the authorship

---

[1] The situation becomes pathetically impossible when men's theological conscience is shocked by the suggestion that Jesus was wrong, and their political conscience by the claim that he should be obeyed.

of the Jewish scriptures.   Just as it was wrong and futile
to pretend that when he said "David said" and quoted a
psalm, he did not mean to ascribe it to David, it is futile
to argue that when he said "resist not evil" and "love
your enemies" he sanctioned the patriotic pursuit of war.

JERUSALEM

FOR the history of the disciples after the death of Jesus we are dependent upon a single source, the Acts of the Apostles, which can, however, be controlled, and to some extent corrected, by the gospels and by the epistles of Paul.

It is now generally recognised that if any one wishes to write a life of Christ he ought to base his work not on the gospels as we have them now, but rather on the information provided by the critical analysis of the gospels as to their sources. These sources, or at least the two oldest and most important, have become well known as Mark and Q. Every one nowaday is aware that behind Matthew and Luke is a document which was almost or entirely identical with our Mark, and that in addition to this both Matthew and Luke used another source, or possibly sources, to which the name of Q is given. In general, however, there is a tendency among those who have acquired this insight into the composition of the gospels from lectures or from little books rather than by the study of a synopsis to attach altogether too rigid an importance to these results.

Mark, though a document of early date and unsurpassed value, is the Greek edition of an earlier Aramaic tradition, probably, though not certainly, in documentary form before it was translated. It would be a miracle if it contained nothing due to the Greek circle in which its present form was produced.

Q, after all, is the name, not of an existing document,

but of the critical judgement that there is a documentary
source behind material common to Matthew and Luke
but absent in Mark. This critical judgement is accepted
by theologians as well as critics; but theologians, with a
distrust of criticism not wholly unjustified, frequently
prefer a mechanical to a rational application of this discovery, and dignify their preference by calling it objective,
though it is difficult to see why a process should be regarded as objective, in any valuable sense of the word,
because it automatically accepts as derived from Q everything common to Matthew and Luke, and leaves out all
the rest. It is merely a method of canonising the subjectivity of Matthew when it agrees with that of Luke,
or of Luke when it agrees with that of Matthew, and
damning both of them when they happen to disagree.
Why the subjectivity of the editors of the gospels becomes
objective when it is accepted by modern writers is a little
difficult to see.

The result of this concentration of attention on the
value of synoptic criticism for the life of Jesus and of
the neglect of the editorial subjectivity of the evangelists
has been a general tendency to overlook the value of the
gospels as the record of the opinion of the generation which
produced them. Yet obviously there are no other documents which tell us the views held in the early Church
of the teaching and office of Christ. On this subject they
give even more information than Acts, and enable us to
control it by showing the gradual development of thought
and language in the Christian community.

Similarly, for a slightly later period and for a different
locality, the Pauline epistles give us glimpses of the
process of development—a process by no means always
peaceable—of which the results are recorded in the second
part of Acts.

In this way the critical use of the gospels, the Acts, and
Pauline epistles enable us to trace the general outline of
the early stages of the synthesis between primitive Jewish

Christianity and the spirit of Graeco-Oriental mysteries. It takes us in succession into Jerusalem, Antioch, and Corinth, not because these were the only churches which grew up in this period, but because it is in the main their tradition which is preserved in the documents at our disposal.

What was the course of events immediately after the death of Jesus? There is no period of which the details are more obscure, but the criticism of Mark and Acts enables us to reconstruct its general outline. The fortunate preservation of Mark enables us to correct the narrative of Acts. If we had Acts alone we should have no doubt but that the disciples stayed in Jerusalem, and settled there from the time when they entered it with Jesus on the first Palm Sunday until the day when they left it to preach to the world outside. Mark, however, is convincing proof that Acts has omitted a complete incident. In Mark xiv. 28 Jesus is represented as saying, "After I am risen I will go before you into Galilee," and in Mark xvi. 7 the young man at the tomb says, "Go tell his disciples and Peter that he goes before you into Galilee, there ye shall see him." The sequence of events clearly implied is that the disciples after the death of Jesus went back to Galilee, where they saw the risen Jesus. Inspired by this vision, they returned to Jerusalem to wait for his return in triumph, and meanwhile to continue the work which he had begun. Unfortunately the end of Mark, which undoubtedly described the details, has disappeared, but the general sequence is as clear as anything can be which is not definitely narrated.

The general tenor of the narrative in Acts makes it plain that in Jerusalem they settled down as a separate synagogue. Any ten Jews had a right to form a synagogue of their own, and general community of interests, joined to opinions differing from those of others, would be the natural basis of its organisation; but it is sometimes

hard for Christians, who have come to think of identity of
opinion, especially on points beyond the reach of proof, as
the basis of ecclesiastical life, to understand that Pales-
tinian Judaism admitted the widest possible range of
thought, and that the Church of Israel rested not on
uniformity of thought, but on obedience to the Law.
Naturally there was in point of fact considerable agreement in opinion, and naturally also difference of opinion
led to quarrels and hostility; but in general the Church
of Israel in the first century was as characteristically based
on uniformity of conduct as the Christian Church in the
fourth and following centuries was based on uniformity
of opinion.

On three points this synagogue of the Nazarenes, as
the disciples were called, differed from other Jews: (1)
They held the opinion that they were inspired, at least
at intervals, by the Spirit of God; (2) they followed a
special kind of communistic rule which they probably
regarded as fulfilling the teaching of Jesus; (3) they held
and preached distinctive opinions about Jesus himself.

The opinion that the disciples were inspired by the
Holy Spirit was in some ways the keystone of Christian
life. It formed a connecting link with the authority of
Jesus himself; for, whatever the later generation of Christians may have thought, it is clear from Mark that Jesus
in his public preaching never claimed the authority of
any special office or function such as that associated with
the word "Messiah" or with the title "Son of Man," even
though he may have allowed an inner ring of disciples to
believe that these were the offices to which he was entitled.
Nor during his lifetime did he even permit his followers
in their preaching to ascribe any such rank to him. The
authority which he actually claimed for his words and
deeds was that of the Holy Spirit of God; and those who
maintained that he cast out demons by the power of Satan
were, he said, guilty of blasphemy against the Holy Spirit.
It is probable that the gospel tradition is trustworthy

which associates his baptism at the hands of John the Baptist with his first consciousness of this inspiration.

Jesus, then, had claimed for himself, openly and publicly, the authority of the Holy Spirit. There is no evidence that any of his disciples had claimed this for themselves during his lifetime, but after his death it seemed to them that the Spirit which had filled their Master had descended on them, inspiring their words and guiding their actions.[1]

What ought to be our verdict on this claim of the first Christians? To see the question in its true light it is necessary to distinguish between the experience of the Christians and the opinion which they held about it. Their opinion was that they had been taken possession of by the Spirit of God, which was acting through them, so that their words and deeds had the authority no longer of fallible man but of the omnipotent and infallible God. This theory was a heritage from a distant past in Israel when the Spirit of the Lord had been regarded as the source of all extraordinary events, good or evil. Later, evil events had no longer been attributed to the Spirit of the Lord, but to demons or unclean spirits who peopled the earth and took possession of men as they found opportunity. To them were attributed disease, misfortune, and especially the raving of madness, while healing and prophecy were attributed to the Divine Spirit.

In modern times we no longer attribute disease, misfortune, or madness to devils, not because these phenomena have ceased, but because we have a different theory of their origin, which, on the whole, produces more satisfactory therapeutic results than the theory of possession. Similarly the phenomena of prophecy, which the Jews ascribed to the Spirit of God, remain. There has never

---

[1] I have discussed the story of the gift of the Spirit at Pentecost in the *Earlier Epistles of St. Paul*, pp. 241 ff., and have added some critical remarks on the various forms of the tradition in the *Prolegomena to Acts*, i. 322 f.

been a generation lacking in men who believe that their action and speech are being governed by a compelling force, separate from the ordinary process of volition. Those who have this experience seem to themselves to be, as it were, the spectators of their own deeds, or to be listening to their own utterances. Under its influence individuals, groups of men, or even nations, are carried away by inexplicable waves of passion or enthusiasm which, once aroused, cannot be resisted till their force is spent. This consciousness has been felt in varying degree in every generation, and the progress of humanity can never be explained unless it be taken into account. Sometimes, in the inevitable reaction after the psychic stress of such experiences, men have resented, doubted, or denied the validity of their own consciousness; sometimes they have regarded it as possessing a value exceeding all else in life. Usually those who have it attract the hostility of their contemporaries, scarcely tempered by the allegiance of a few followers, and their names are forgotten in a few years, but sometimes the verdict of contemporary hatred is reversed by posterity, which endeavours to compensate by legendary honours for the contempt and contumely of life.

The problem presented by this experience is really twofold. It calls for a judgement as to its origin and for a judgement as to its value, and on neither point has there as yet been sufficiently clear discussion.

Does the experience of controlling force which the prophet feels really come from some external influence, or is it merely his consciousness of ordinarily unknown depths in his own nature? It is obvious that a theory of prophecy could be made on lines rendered familiar by psychologists, by suggesting that what happens in a prophetic experience is the sudden "coming up" of what is ordinarily "subliminal." It is, however, important to remember that this is merely a modern hypothesis, just as the Jewish view of inspiration was an ancient one. But it is impossible in a rational theology to combine fragments of two wholly different explanations of life and of the universe. "The Spirit" was an admirably intelligible phrase in the Jewish or early Christian view of the universe; it does not fit in well with the modern view of the universe. Similarly the theory of subliminal action fits very well into the modern view, but not into that of traditional Christian theology. Preachers seem to make a serious mistake when they try to combine the language of two rival hypotheses to explain the same human experience.

The judgement of value which ought to be passed on the prophets is no clearer than the judgement of origin. The early Church knew perfectly well that there were true prophets and false prophets,[1] and so did the Jews, but in the end the only way of distinguishing them was to say that a true prophet was a prophet who was right, and a false prophet was a prophet who was wrong. Nor can we arrive at any different judgement. The truth is,— and unfortunately the modern world is sometimes in danger of forgetting it,—that the difference between right and wrong, fact and fancy, possibility and impossibility, is inherent in the nature of things and incapable of modification by human beings, prophets or otherwise. It cannot be changed by the glowing utterances of poets, prophets, or preachers, or by the unanimous votes of peoples. All that man can do is to discover it and obey it with humility. The mere fact of discovery arouses in some men an emotion which for the moment seems to change their being, but their emotion does not change or increase the truth, and it may be questioned whether in some cases it has not prevented them from seeing rightly the value of what they have found. For the same deep emotion is sometimes caused by error, and there are few mistakes

[1] I have discussed the history of early Christian attempts to distinguish false from true prophets in "De strijd tusschen het oudste Christendom en de bedriegers" in the *Theologisch Tijdschrift*, xlii. 395-411.

more deadly than to judge the truth of what a man says, or the value of what he does, by the emotion which he feels himself—however sincerely—or arouses in others—however vehemently.

The way of life which the first Christians adopted was especially marked by an attempt to organise themselves on communistic principles. The Christians shared all things; those who had property realised it, and pooled the proceeds in a common fund, which was distributed to individual members as need arose. It is impossible not to recognise in this action consistent and literal obedience to the teaching of Jesus. The disciples had followed Jesus to the end of his journey in Jerusalem; they were waiting for his manifestation in glory, and sold all that they had and gave to the poor. But in terms of political economy the Church was realising the capital of its members and living on the division of the proceeds. It is not surprising that under these circumstances for the moment none was in need among them, and that they shared their food in gladness of heart, for nothing so immediately relieves necessity or creates gladness of heart as living on capital, which would be indeed an ideal system of economy if society were coming to an end, or capital were not. It is probable that the Church thought that society would soon end, but it proved to be wrong, and it is not surprising that the same book, which in its early chapters relates the remarkable lack of poverty among the Christians, has in the end to describe the generous help sent by the Gentile churches to the poor brethren.

We may, however, surmise that the breakdown of this communistic experiment was accompanied by other difficulties in the Church. It appears that by this time Christianity had attracted the favourable attention of a number of Jews who belonged at least by origin to the Diaspora, and this introduced a new element, destined in the end to become dominant and much more objectionable than the original disciples to the Jews of Jerusalem. We know from other sources that among the Hellenistic Jews was a tendency to liberalism, or Hellenism. This touched the Jews where they were most sensitive, for it affected not opinion but conduct, and seemed to threaten the destruction of the Jewish Law. They were apparently willing to tolerate Peter and the rest, so long as they confined themselves to holding peculiar opinions about the Messiah, and remained perfectly orthodox in their fulfilment of all the requirements of the Law. But when the synagogue of the Nazarenes took to themselves Hellenists the situation became intolerable: a severe persecution arose, Stephen was killed, and the rest of the Hellenistic party were driven out of Jerusalem, though the original disciples remained, for the time at least, in comparative peace. The Hellenists scattered throughout the Gentile neighbourhood of Palestine, and their future history will have to be considered later.

The opinion which the disciples held of Jesus now became part of their preaching in a manner which had not been the case during his lifetime. To distinguish its nature and development requires a somewhat critical investigation of the meaning and history of the titles first used in speaking of Jesus. The chief of these are Messiah, Son of Man, Son of God, and Servant. That which in the end was the most important of all—Lord—was probably not used until a little later.

Messiah is really an adjective which, translated literally, means "anointed," or in Greek Χριστος, but whereas to say that a man was anointed has no more meaning in Greek than it has in English, it had in Hebrew the clear and universally understood meaning of "consecrated" or "appointed by God." It was applied in the Old Testament to the high-priest, and it is habitually used in this sense in the Mishna. It was also used of Saul, of David, and of some of the other kings, but always with some defining phrase attached to it, generally speaking "the anointed of Jehovah." Without definition it is not found until

the Christian period. There is no reason to suppose that
at the beginning of the first century it was used exclusively to describe the hope of the Jews that a prince of
the house of David would restore their fallen fortunes,
though in the later Jewish literature it was used in this
way.[1]

Thus if we try to construct the impression which the
early Christians made on the Jews of Jerusalem by claim-
ing that Jesus was anointed by God, we are obliged to
say that the phrase itself only implied his divine appointment; it did not by itself indicate definitely the function
to which he was appointed. But the way in which it was
used must have suggested two special functions—that of
the Davidic prince alluded to above, and that of the supernatural representative of God who would judge the world
at the last day.

It is quite clear that the writer of Luke and Acts, and
the editor of Matthew, identified Jesus with the expected
Son of David, but there is room for doubt whether this
fully represents the thought of the first disciples. There
is very little in Mark which identifies Jesus with the Son
of David. In the preaching of Jesus the Kingdom of
God, so far as it was not the divine sovereignty, was the
Age to Come much more than the restored monarchy. It
is true that the people of Jerusalem seem to have been
looking forward to a Davidic king, as may be seen from
the cries of the multitude at the entry of Jesus into
Jerusalem. It is also true that Bartimaeus greeted Jesus
as Son of David; but there is nothing in the recorded
words of Jesus to show that he accepted this view. It
seems, therefore, probable that just as the people were
thinking of the splendours of a restored monarchy, while
Jesus was speaking of the reign of God in the Age to
Come, so they were looking for a Davidic Messiah, and

[1] The history of the phrase in the Old Testament and in Jewish
literature is discussed by G. F. Moore in the *Prolegomena to Acts*,
pp. 346 ff.

explained Jesus' strange and overmastering personality in accordance with their own wishes rather than with his words. It is not the only point at which the Church followed the leading of the people rather than the teaching of Jesus.

The figure of the Son of Man destined to be God's representative at the day of judgement which will divide this age from the Age to Come is prominent in the undoubted teaching of Jesus, but forms one of the most difficult problems in New Testament criticism. There seems but little doubt that "Son of Man," which in Greek is an unintelligible phrase rather than a title, was quite as obscure to the generation of Greek Christians which produced the present gospels as it is to ourselves. It was to them merely the strange self-designation of Jesus. Probably the editors of the gospels believed that Jesus used this phrase continually, and introduced it into their redactions of early sources without stopping too narrowly to inquire either whether it had this meaning in the passage in question, or whether the way in which they were using it was consistent with the connotation of the phrase. The result is that both in Mark and in Q there are passages in which "Son of Man" represents an Aramaic phrase which might be translated literally in this way, but would be idiomatically rendered "man." For instance, it is tolerably certain that in the passage in which Jesus speaks of the Sabbath and says, "The Sabbath was made for man and not man for the Sabbath," he really continued, "so that man is lord also of the Sabbath," but in unidiomatic translation the word meaning "man" was rendered "Son of Man" and interpreted as referring to Jesus himself. The reason for saying that this is tolerably certain is that the only alternative is that "Son of Man" really meant "Jesus," and was intended as a reference to the "Son of Man" who plays a part in some of the apocalypses, and it seems inconceivable that Jesus, who forbade his disciples to tell the public that he was the Messiah, could so openly have claimed this dignity.

Discussion of the phrase "Son of Man" has been going on for many years, and has made it increasingly clear that, apart from the unidiomatic translations referred to above, apocalyptic usage is the most important factor in the problem. An obscure but impressive passage in Daniel was taken up in the Book of Enoch, which describes in the Similitudes the vision of a Man—or in Aramaic phraseology a "Son of Man"—in heaven, who was "anointed," that is to say consecrated by God, to act as the judge at the end of the age. Jesus appears to have used this expression, and to have anticipated the speedy coming in judgement of this Man on the clouds of heaven. This much may be regarded as agreed upon by all investigators. But the curious and striking thing is that in none of the Marcan passages in which it is used in this sense does it unambiguously refer to Jesus himself. No doubt the disciples were convinced that it did, but it is therefore all the more interesting and important that his actual words as reported by them do not necessarily confirm their opinion. On the other hand, there is a series of passages peculiar to Mark (that is to say, none of them is found in Q) in which "Son of Man" does not refer to any coming in judgement, but to the approaching passion, death, and resurrection of Jesus. If he really uttered these words, beyond doubt he meant himself by the Son of Man, and was introducing an entirely unparalleled and new element into the delineation of this supernatural figure. But did he use these words? In the description of the passion, death, and resurrection it is generally recognised that the exactness of the prediction probably owes something to the disciples' later knowledge of the actual course of events. Their conduct at the arrest of Jesus, and the entire absence of any sign of expectation of the resurrection, render it very improbable that Jesus spoke with the definiteness ascribed to him. In this case, therefore, there is decided reason for thinking that the phrase "Son of Man" may itself belong to the embellishment rather than to the body of tradition.

Thus the passages in which Jesus certainly uses "Son of Man" are ambiguous—they need not necessarily refer to him, and the passages which unambiguously refer to him were not certainly spoken by him. For this reason it is somewhat more probable than not that the identification of Jesus with the Son of Man was not made by Jesus himself. But it certainly embodies the earliest opinion of the disciples concerning him, and it is in all probability to this apocalyptic figure of the Man in heaven, predestined to judge the world and anointed by God for that purpose, that the Marcan tradition (we cannot speak with certainty of Q) referred when it described Jesus as "anointed."

A little later the circles represented by Matthew and Luke added to this the more popular expectation of the restored monarchy of the house of David; but the original stamp was never lost, and the functions of the Christian Messiah, as apart from his name, were always those of the Man of Enoch, much more than those of the Davidic king of the Psalms of Solomon.

Finally, the concept of the Man who was to judge the world was extensively modified by the actual course of the passion, death, and resurrection of Jesus, and the Lukan writings, though probably not Mark, Q, or even Matthew, facilitated or confirmed this process by connecting the story of Jesus with the picture given in the fifty-third chapter of Isaiah of the suffering of the righteous Servant of the Lord.

The Servant is a comparatively common title in the Old Testament for those who faithfully carried out the will of God; it is used of Abraham, David, and Job among the sons of Israel, of Cyrus among the heathen, of Israel in general, and of the righteous portion of Israel in particular. In some parts, but not in all, the suffering of the Servant, whoever he may be, is emphasised; but there is no trace in the Old Testament, or in the later Jewish writings, that these descriptions were regarded as predictive of the future. It was inevitable that the resemblance of the death of Jesus to Isaiah liii. should sooner or later strike Christian readers of the Old Testament, but it does not appear to have done so immediately, and it is doubtful whether Isaiah liii. was the first "suffering" passage in the Old Testament to be ascribed to him. It is more probable that the use of the twenty-second Psalm was earlier.

One further title of Jesus in the early Christian literature remains to be discussed. He is referred to as Son of God. What would this phrase mean in Jewish ears? In general the Jews regarded God as unique. The idea of a Son of God in any physical sense, such as seemed natural enough to the heathen world, would have been unthinkable to them, but they believed that God himself had used the phrase metaphorically to describe the relation between him and his chosen people. It was a moral sonship, not a physical one in the heathen sense, or a metaphysical one in the later Christian sense.

In the later literature the phrase developed on two separate lines. There was the tendency, exemplified in some of the Psalms, and still more in the Psalms of Solomon, to use the phrase "Son of God" to describe the Davidic king, but it was also used in quite a different sense in the Wisdom Literature as the description of the righteous man, and especially of the righteous man who suffered.

In Christian literature it seems tolerably clear that the history of the phrase passed through several stages. The latest, though in the end the most important for the development of doctrine, is that of metaphysical sonship, which followed upon the equation of "Son of God" with "Logos." Somewhat earlier than this, in the early chapters of Luke, and probably of Matthew, is an idea of sonship which approximates to the physical notion of the heathen world. Earlier still it was probably used as a synonym for the Davidic Messiah. The question is whether this is its meaning in the earliest passage of all,—the account given in the first chapter of Mark of the voice from heaven at the baptism which said, "Thou art my beloved Son in whom I am well pleased." It is generally held that this is a quotation from the second Psalm,[1] and therefore identifies Jesus with the Davidic Messiah. But is it quite so certain that it is a quotation from anything? The words of the Psalm are really quite different, "Thou art my Son" instead of "Beloved Son," and "This day have I begotten thee" instead of "in whom I am well pleased." Why should we suppose either that the voice from heaven was restricted to quoting scripture, or that it did so with quite remarkable inaccuracy? If, however, the idea be abandoned that the voice from heaven necessarily refers to the second Psalm, it becomes an open question whether Jesus himself regarded his divine sonship as the Davidic messiahship, or as that divine sonship which the Book of Wisdom ascribes to the righteous. The problem thus raised can never be settled, for the evidence is insufficient; but neither can it be dismissed, for it is implicit in the gospel itself.

The whole importance of this series of problems in the history of early Christology is often strangely mistaken. It seems to many as though the line of thought suggested above, which reduces to a vanishing point the amount of Christology traceable, in the ordinary sense of the word, to Jesus himself, is in some way a grave loss to Christianity. No doubt it is a departure from orthodoxy. But if the history of religion has any clear lesson, it is that a nearer approach to truth is always a departure from orthodoxy. Moreover, the alternative to the view

[1] W. C. Allen is a noteworthy exception. See his note on Matt. iii. 17 in the *International Critical Commentary*. See further *Prolegomena to Acts*, pp. 397 ff.

stated above is to hold that Jesus did regard himself as either one or both of the two Jewish figures, the Davidic Messiah and the Son of Man described in Enoch. Both of these are part of a general view of the universe, and especially of a prognostication of the future, wholly different from our own, and quite incredible to modern minds. How do we endanger the future of Christianity by doubting that Jesus identified himself with figures central in incredible and now almost universally abandoned forms of thought?

III

ANTIOCH

ACCORDING to Acts the result of the persecution of Stephen was the spread of Christianity outside Palestine. As the narrative stands it seems to imply that before this time there had been no Christian propaganda outside Jerusalem. But significant details show that this impression is wrong and merely due to the fact that the writer gives no account of the earlier stages.

After the death of Stephen Paul appears to have continued his persecuting zeal, and obtained authority to go to Damascus and prosecute the Christians resident there. Obviously, then, the Christian movement had already spread to Damascus, but there is no hint in Acts as to how it did so. That in so doing it had advanced beyond the limits of the Synagogue is not clear, but Damascus was essentially a Gentile city, and the following considerations suggest that it had done so. We know that the Jews of the Diaspora at this period were filled with a proselytising zeal of which the fact is more certain than the details. It is also tolerably plain from Philo that there was a strong tendency to Hellenise and go further than orthodox Jews were willing to tolerate. It is also certain that the outcry against the Christians in Jerusalem which led to the death of Stephen did not start among the native Jews but among the Hellenists—those who belonged to the synagogues of the freedmen and of the Cyrenaeans, Alexandrians, Cilicians, and Asians, who

had synagogues in Jerusalem.[1] In addition to this,
though Acts suggests that the origin of the Seven was the
necessity of administering the funds of the community,
it is clear that in point of fact it was their preaching
which made them prominent. Finally, it is clear from
Acts that Philip began to preach to the Gentiles as soon
as he left Jerusalem, and that some of the Cypriots and
Cyrenaeans did the same.

There is thus considerable though not overwhelming
evidence that preaching to the Gentiles began somewhat
sooner than is popularly supposed, and that before the
conversion of Paul near Damascus by the vision of the
risen Lord, or before the conversion of Peter by the episode of Cornelius, there was already a Christian mission
to the Gentiles. The importance of this is that it enables
us to see the history of the early Church in a somewhat
different perspective. It shows that Paul was not the
first, though he was undoubtedly the greatest, of the Christians who preached to the Gentiles. He was a part of
Hellenistic Christianity, and probably, as will be seen
later, not the most extreme of its adherents.

We have, then, to imagine the gradual rise of a Hellenising movement among the Christians, of which the Seven
were probably the original leaders in Jerusalem, while unknown disciples, of whom we only know that they were
successful in Damascus, were carrying it on in other places.
The Twelve appear to have regarded the movement with
doubt and suspicion, and the Jews in Jerusalem always
distinguished between the original disciples and the Hellenists. Gradually, however, the opposition of the Twelve
and their followers crumbled away. The final defection,
from the point of view of Judaism, was that of Peter.
To judge from Acts he had undertaken a mission in
Palestine, following up the work of Philip and probably

---

[1] It is probable that Paul was at this time settled in Damascus
rather than Jerusalem. If so, which synagogue in Jerusalem did
he frequent? That of the Cilicians as a native of Tarsus?

of others, but the story brings to notice one of the characteristic weaknesses of Acts as history. It always omits or minimises differences of opinion and quarrels among Christians. We know this by comparing the Epistles with the Acts. It is therefore perfectly legitimate to suppose that there may well have been far more friction at first between the Hellenist missionaries and the Twelve than Acts suggests. But in the end Peter had a vision at Joppa which convinced him that he was wrong, and he accepted Cornelius as a brother Christian. Acts would have us understand that the whole Church at Jerusalem accepted Peter's position, but in view of the Judaistic controversy, which continued to rage much later than this time, it is certain that this is not in accordance with fact. It is significant that soon after this Peter was put in prison, and on his escape from prison left Jerusalem.[1]

From this time on, if not before, the undoubted head of the Church in Jerusalem was James, the brother of the Lord. What was his attitude towards the Hellenising Christians? Acts would have us understand that he was always on perfectly good terms with Peter, and later on with Paul. But that is hardly the impression given by the Pauline epistles, which very clearly distinguish Peter from James and his emissaries. Paul's view is that Peter was in principle on the same side as himself, and that he therefore had no right to yield to the representatives of James; but he never suggests that James and he were on the same side. Nor had the Jews in Jerusalem any illusions on the subject; when Paul appeared in the temple he was promptly arrested, but not until the popular madness of the year 66 did any of the orthodox Jews think of interfering with James, the head of the Christians in Jerusalem.

Thus Acts plainly has understated the amount of controversy between the Hellenising Christians and the origi-

[1] Unless this story is misplaced and ought to come before Acts ix. 32.

nal community. Failure to see this is due to the ultimately complete triumph of the Hellenistic party, who
naturally looked on what was really the conservative position as Judaising, whereas the truth was that they themselves were Hellenising.

According to Acts the most successful centre of Hellenistic Christianity was Antioch. Here, too, it is possible that the picture presented by it is one-sided, owing
to the fact that, at least in many places, Acts reproduces
the tradition of Antioch. Doubtless there were other
centres equally important. Neither Ephesus nor Rome
seems to have been founded by missionaries from Antioch,
though Paul and the other Antiochean missionaries came
into their history at an early date.

The controversy between the school of James and the
Hellenistic Christians appears to have been very acute in
Antioch, but the details are extremely obscure. Acts represents the beginning of the Church at Antioch as due
to Hellenistic Christians who left Jerusalem after the
death of Stephen. Nor is there any reason to doubt the
correctness of this tradition, which is probably that of
Antioch itself. A little later Barnabas came down from
Jerusalem to Antioch. Acts does not state, but seems to
imply, that he came down, as Peter had come to Samaria,
in order to criticise and control Hellenistic enthusiasm.
But, like Peter at Caesarea, he was converted by the Hellenists, and stayed to help their mission. He went further than this: hearing apparently of the success of Paul
at Tarsus he sent for him and co-opted him into the service
of the Church at Antioch. It is worth noting in passing
that the complete absence of any details as to Paul's work
in Tarsus, and the silence concerning his movements from
the time he left Jerusalem soon after his conversion, proves
that this part of Acts is an Antiochean rather than a
Pauline tradition.

Soon after this more missionaries arrived from Jerusalem. They do not appear to have been active propa-

gandists, but brought with them a sad story of approaching destitution in the famine which was at hand. The
Church at Antioch rose to the necessity and sent Paul
and Barnabas with relief.[1] Acts tells us nothing more
of what happened, but that soon after Paul and Barnabas,
having returned to Antioch, started on the "First Missionary Journey." [2]   On their return, however, a mission
of protest against their methods arrived from Jerusalem.
Paul, Barnabas, and some others went up to Jerusalem;
a meeting of the representatives of the two churches was
held, and an amicable agreement which was in the main
a triumph for Antioch was arrived at.[3]

This appears to be Paul's third visit to Jerusalem after
his conversion; but this raises difficulties, and has led
to considerable critical investigation and not a little controversy. It had always been supposed that this visit of
Paul to Jerusalem was identical with that described in the
second chapter of Galatians, but in that chapter Paul,
calling God to witness that he is not lying, makes a statement which loses all its point if it was not his second visit.
Various attempts to explain this difficulty have been made.
One solution of the problem is that the visit to Jerusalem
described in Galatians ii. is not identical with that of
Acts xv., but is an episode connected with the visit in the
time of the famine relief, which the writer of Acts had
either not known or thought it unnecessary to recount.[4]
According to this theory the visit described in Acts xv.
took place after the visit in Galatians had been written.
But this theory does not answer the difficulty that the
apostolic decrees are not mentioned in the Epistles to the
Corinthians, and that it is incredible that they could have
been overlooked by Paul if the account in Acts xv. were

[1] Acts xi. 27 ff.
[2] Acts xii. 25–xiv. 28.
[3] Acts xv.
[4] See especially C. W. Emmet, *The Eschatological Question in the
Gospels and other Studies*, pp. 191 ff., and K. Lake, *The Earlier
Epistles of St. Paul*, pp. 274 ff.

wholly correct. It seems better to accept the suggestion
that the solution of the problem is to be found in the
source-criticism of Acts.

The source-criticism of Acts has passed through three
more or less spasmodic stages.[1] The first was early in the
nineteenth century when a number of scholars endeavoured to analyse the book. Their efforts were not very
successful, though they unearthed a great many interesting phenomena. Later on, in the 'nineties, another series
of efforts were made with, on the whole, even less success
than before. Finally, in our own time there have been
some interesting suggestions by Harnack, Schwartz, and
Torrey.[2]

The last named has shown extremely good reason for
thinking that there is an Aramaic source behind the first
fifteen chapters of Acts.[3] He is less convincing when he
tries to prove that this was a single document, and that it
was faithfully translated without addition or change by
the editor of Acts. It seems more probable that there was
more than one Aramaic source, and that it was often
changed and interpolated by the editor.

Harnack skilfully tries to distinguish two main lines
of tradition, that of Antioch and that of Jerusalem. He

[1] The most important names in the first period are Königsmann,
Schleiermacher, Gfrörer, and Schwanbeck, especially the last; in the
second period B. Weiss, Wendt, Sorof, Jüngst, J. Weiss, Spitta,
Clemen, Hilgenfeld. In general the work of this group is inferior
in value to that of their predecessors. A clear and invaluable sum-
mary of both is given by W. Heitmuller in the *Theologische Rund-
schau* for 1899, pp. 47 ff.

[2] Perhaps Norden's name should be added, but interesting and
stimulating though his book *Agnostos Theos* be, it suffers from igno-
rance of early Christianity, and has little permanent value for the
criticism of Acts.

[3] A. von Harnack, *Untersuchungen zu den Schriften des Lukas;*
E. Schwartz, "Zur Chronologie des Paulus," in the *Göttingische
Nachrichten*, 1907, pp. 263 ff.; C. C. Torrey, "The Composition and
Date of Acts," in the *Harvard Theological Studies*, i. The most
damaging criticism of Torrey is that of F. C. Burkitt in the *Journal
of Theological Studies*, Oct. 1919, but I do not think that he
answers Torrey's case.

also thinks the Jerusalem tradition existed in two forms, which can be distinguished as doublets in Acts i.-v. He attaches Acts xv. to the tradition of Antioch, but it seems more probable that it belongs to the Jerusalem tradition. The truth may be as follows: soon after the time when Barnabas had gone over to the Hellenistic party another body of Christians from Jerusalem came to Antioch. In the years which followed there grew up two traditions of what happened next. The tradition at Antioch was that the Christians from Jerusalem had been chiefly concerned with the physical necessities of their Church, though they were undoubtedly men possessed of a prophetic gift. They had so worked on the sympathy of Antioch that it had accepted the needs of the poor saints in Jerusalem as a responsibility laid on it by heaven. This tradition is preserved in a short form in Acts xi., and in the Epistle to the Galatians Paul energetically sustained its correctness, incidentally mentioning some other events connected with his stay at Jerusalem, the perversion of which, as he maintained, had given rise to the tradition of Jerusalem. This latter tradition the editor of Acts had found preserved in the document which he has used as the basis of Acts xv., and if any one will read Galatians ii. alongside of Acts xv., not in order to see how much they agree or differ, but rather to note how far they might be different accounts of the same series of events, he will see that Paul's chief contention is that he only saw the leaders of the community at Jerusalem in private, and that they at no time succeeded in imposing any regulations on him. The vigour of his protestations seems to indicate that his opponents had maintained that the meeting was an official one, and that it had imposed regulations, namely, should the theory which is being suggested be correct, the Apostolic Decrees.

The two traditions are naturally quite contradictory; but human nature is so constituted that it is not impossible for two sets of people, especially after some lapse of

time, to give entirely different accounts of the same events
and to do so in perfectly good faith. The editor of Acts,
however, did not realise that the two traditions referred
to the same event, and made a mistake in thinking that
the meeting which he found described in the Jerusalem
source came after and not before the first missionary
journey. Ed. Schwartz goes further. He points out
that the first missionary journey follows the account of
the meeting in Jerusalem given in Acts xi., and that the
second journey follows the account given in Acts xv. If
there was really only one meeting, was there not really
only one journey, which the editor of Acts, or his sources,
converted into two?

However this may be, and no agreement among critics
is ever likely to be reached, it is at least certain that there
was considerable friction between Jerusalem and Antioch,
and that Antioch wholly refused to accept the dictation
of Jerusalem. On the contrary, it undertook wide-reach-
ing missions, of one of which Paul became the leader,
founding churches in Galatia, Asia, and Achaea. Of his
career we have an obviously good account, so far as the
sequence of events is concerned, in the second part of
Acts, and some interesting sidelights on its difficulties and
trials in the Pauline epistles.

What were the main characteristics of the preaching
to the Gentiles which thus found a centre in Antioch?
Its basis was the intellectual heritage from Jerusalem
which made the Christians teach that the God of the Jews
was the only true God, and that Jesus had been appointed
by him as the Man who would judge the world at the end
of the age. This represents the teaching in Marcan tradition as to the Son of Man, but Paul also accepted the view
that Jesus was the Son of David, though he seems to have
eliminated the purely national character of the expected
restoration of the kingdom of the Jews under a Davidic
king.

The only complete evidence as to the exact form of the

expectation which played a part in the teaching of Paul, and presumably in that of the Church of Antioch as a whole, is the invaluable description given in the Epistles [1] of the sequence of events to which Paul looked forward. According to this he expected that Jesus would come on the clouds of heaven; Christians who had died would be raised up, and the rest would be changed, so that they would no longer consist of flesh and blood, but of spirit. But, just as in 4 Ezra, the reign of the Messiah is limited; a time will come when he will deliver up his dominion to God. Then comes "the End," and Paul takes the picture no further. Is it too much to suppose that, like 4 Ezra, he thought that at the End the whole of the present order would cease, and that after it would come the general resurrection and judgement, to which he frequently alludes, followed by the life of the Age to Come? In any case the idea of the limited reign of the Messiah, and the increased emphasis on the descent of Jesus from David, are points of contact with 4 Ezra, and thus make it increasingly possible that Paul thought that the resurrection of Christians to life would be separate from the final resurrection of all to judgement.

This original Christian teaching was essentially Jewish, but much of the phraseology in which it would have been expressed by Jews must have been unintelligible to Greek ears. It therefore soon either disappeared or was transformed. The Kingdom of God, for instance, is as rarely mentioned in the Pauline epistles as it is frequent in the earliest part of the gospels. The word "Christ," translating the Hebrew adjective "anointed," was entirely unintelligible to Greek ears, and became a proper name. "Son of Man" or "Man" would have been even more unintelligible; Paul never used "Son of Man," and it is doubtful whether he uses the word "Man" in the technical apocalyptic sense. But though the words were unintelligible the ideas had not disappeared. The functions

[1] Especially 1 Cor. xv. and 1 Thess. iv.

attributed to the Son of Man in the gospels still remain attributed to Jesus in the Pauline epistles, though they are scarcely so much emphasised.

The Antiochean missionaries seem to have adopted a new word to take the place of the unintelligible "Messiah" and "Son of Man," and called Jesus "Lord." It is made tolerably certain by comparing the oldest strata of the gospels with the more recent that this word was not used in Jerusalem or in Galilee as a title of Jesus. It may have been used occasionally in Aramaic-speaking circles, but it became dominant in Greek. Its extreme importance is that it was already familiar to the Greek-speaking world in connection with religion. It had become the typical title for the God of one of the Graeco-Oriental cults which offered private salvation [1] to individuals. It was therefore inevitable that whatever the Jews may have meant when they called Jesus Lord, their Greek converts interpreted it in the sense in which the word had become familiar to them, and thought in consequence that Jesus was the divine head of a cult by which each individual might obtain salvation. The full importance of this became obvious in a purely Greek centre such as Corinth, but the process began in Antioch.

This change in the significance attached to Jesus had its correlative effect on the position which the Christians ascribed to themselves. They came inevitably to regard themselves as the members of a new cult which was superior to all others. Only by joining their number was salvation to be found. In this sense they began to interpret the phrase "Kingdom of God," which in many parts of the gospels very obviously means the Christian Church. Few things, however, are more certain than that Jesus had no intention of founding a new society outside the Jewish Church, and none of these passages can with any probability be ascribed to him, even though at least one

[1] See p. 58.

can, on mechanical grounds, make out a fair case for inclusion in Q.

A correlative change was introduced into the attitude adopted towards the Old Testament. The Antiochean Christians refused to accept it as an obligatory law of conduct; but more and more was it interpreted as prophetic of Jesus, and not only of him but also of the Christian Church. In this way everything that was said of ancient Israel, and all the promises made to it, were transferred to the Christians, who claimed that they, and not the Jews, were the ancient People of God. The complete fulfilment of this process did not, it is true, take place in the time of Paul, but it was not long in coming, and even in the epistles there are many places which show that the Christians regarded themselves as the true heirs of the promise.

This transference of the Jewish scriptures to the Christian Church was probably almost as important for the future history of Christianity as the change which made Jesus the centre of a cult offering private salvation, instead of the prophetic herald of the Kingdom of Heaven, destined by God to be his representative at the End of the Age. It meant that Christianity shared with Judaism the advantage, which no other religion in the Empire had, of being a religion with a Book. Nevertheless the obvious fact that the Book was not originally Christian was destined in the long run to lead to considerable difficulty. Though the Old Testament is not always susceptible of the meaning given to it by Jewish rabbis, it is essentially a Jewish book, and the attempt to find in it a series of prophecies foretelling the coming of Jesus was radically wrong. It could not be supported by any straightforward interpretation, which gave to the Old Testament its original historical meaning. The result was the inevitable growth of an unnatural symbolical interpretation which had little difficulty in extracting anything from anything. It is difficult to estimate whether the result has been more good or evil. It produced good, in that it very soon necessitated the growth of a Christian canon—the New Testament added to the Old—and this preserved much great literature for the advantage of future generations, and was a check upon extravagances of thought. Perhaps most important of all, it provided an ethical standard which successive generations of Christians have never succeeded in practising. They have indeed frequently tried to explain away the contrast between their scriptures and their deeds when it became too oppressive, but they have never quite succeeded, or been able entirely to satisfy themselves by these methods: the letter of scripture has constantly remained a salutary protest against the interpretation put upon it. All this has been of enormous advantage for the Christian Church. But on the other hand the infallibility ascribed to the Bible has been an easy weapon for obscurantism, and a drag on intellectual progress. It has prevented the Church from adopting the discoveries of science and criticism in such a way as to make them applicable to religious life. Bible Christianity [1] in some of its more recent forms has become a serious danger, and in moments of depression a student is apt to ask whether in the irony of history the Bible, which strengthened and supported the Church in its early history, and helped it in many generations to moral reformation, is destined to become an instrument for preventing the adaptation of Christianity to the needs of to-day, and to drive the spirit of religion, which is eternal, from organised Christianity to take refuge once more in some newer forms, more receptive of truth, and less tenacious of error.

[1] The reference is to certain American institutions, connected in the main with evangelising movements.

IV

CORINTH

CHRISTIANITY had been profoundly changed by its passage from Galilee to Jerusalem. Whereas the teaching of Jesus had been the announcement of the kingdom of God, the illustration of its character, and the insistent call to men to repent, the central teaching of the disciples in Jerusalem became the claim that Jesus was the Messiah. But the passage from Jerusalem to Antioch had produced still greater changes. After all, the teaching of the disciples in Jerusalem contained no elements foreign to Judaism. It was probably considered by the Jewish authorities as the erroneous application to Jesus of opinions which, rightly or wrongly, were widely held among the Jews; but nothing in it represented concession to Hellenism. As soon as Hellenism was suspected the Christians were at once driven out. In Antioch, on the other hand, much that was distinctly Jewish was abandoned, and Hellenistic thought adopted, so that Jesus became the divine centre of a cult. It is incredible that he should have been so regarded by the Jews of Jerusalem; it is impossible that he should not have been by Gentiles.

It is remarkable that Paul and the other Antiochean missionaries were willing to accept this development, and to make themselves the enthusiastic agents of its propaganda; but they clearly did so, and the point is of extreme importance for the history of Judaism.[1] The only alternative to large concessions to the position of the Dutch

[1] See C. Montefiore, *Judaism and St. Paul.*

radicals is to admit that in the Diaspora the Hellenising of Jews had proceeded more rapidly and far deeper than has as a rule been supposed.

The result is clear, however obscure the process may be; Christianity became a Graeco-Oriental cult, offering salvation, just as did the other mystery religions. It competed with them for the right of succession to the official religion of Rome, and ultimately it triumphed. To understand the situation it is necessary to comprehend the general nature of these cults, and to see the points of likeness and difference in Christianity.

In general all the mystery religions assumed the existence of a Lord, who had passed through various experiences on earth, and finally been glorified and exalted. He had left behind the secret of obtaining the same reward, in the form partly of knowledge, partly of magical ceremonies. His followers knew this secret, and admitted into it those whom the Lord was willing to accept. The initiated obtained protection in this world, and a blessed immortality after death. The Lord was probably not usually identified with the Supreme God; for instance, in Mithraism the Sun, not Mithras, was originally the supreme God, though in the last stages of the cult the difference between the two was apparently blurred, and Mithras became indistinguishable from the Sun.

The Christianity revealed in 1 Corinthians clearly conforms to this type. It has its Lord, Jesus, who is far more than human, but is not identified with the supreme God "the Father"; [1] he has suffered on earth, but been glorified and exalted, and Christians who accept him in faith, and are initiated into the Church by the sacrament of Baptism, obtain a share in his glory, and will enjoy a blessed immortality. The general resemblance is striking and undeniable. It may be summarised, as was said above, by the statement that Christianity offered men salvation, and was believed to fulfil its offer. Indeed, its

[1] 1 Cor. viii. 6.

success was partly due not to any difference from the other cults, but to the fact that it made more exclusive claims, combined with a higher ethical standard, than any other.

But what exactly was meant by salvation? No single answer can be given. In one sense salvation was primarily an eschatological concept, though its formulation was different among Jewish-minded and Greek-minded believers. The Jew meant, in the main, that, at the great day when the dead would rise and join the living before the judgement seat of God, he would be safe from the Divine Wrath, be acquitted, and have a place among those who would live in happiness in the Age to Come. The Greek probably thought rather that each soul which was saved would pass at death to a happier and better existence. Ultimately these two strands of eschatology were woven together, though scarcely reconciled, in the elaborate fabric of the Catholic system of purgatory, paradise, resurrection, judgement, heaven and hell.

In another sense salvation meant something different, which was not eschatological. In accordance with the general spirit of the Graeco-Oriental mysteries, there existed a belief that through sacraments men could change their nature, be born again, and—as Irenaeus puts it—become the children of the eternal and unchangeable God instead of the children of mortal man.[1] In this way they passed, even before death, into eternal life, and they were raised to an existence beyond the reach of Fate. The basis of this concept was doubtless astral, and at least some early Christians believed that whereas the unbaptized were subject to the inimical decrees of the stars, the regenerate were immune.

Judged by our standards this belief is magical, just as the Jewish eschatology is mythological. Neither has part or lot in modern thinking; this does not necessarily prove that they are wrong, but it means that the problem for us is not one of details, but of opposing systems, the parts of

[1] Irenaeus, *Apostolic Preaching*, p. 3.

which cannot be interchanged. We can, with logical propriety, accept the Graeco-Jewish eschatology or the Graeco-Oriental sacramental regeneration if we reject modern thought. But we cannot, except in intellectual chaos, combine the two, or appropriately express modern thought in language belonging to the ancient systems.

The modern man does not believe in any form of salvation known to ancient Christianity. He does believe that so long as life lasts, and he does not know of any limit to its duration, good and evil are realities, and those who do good, and are good, achieve life of increasingly higher and higher potentiality. If anything were gained in practical life by calling this "salvation," it would be right and wise to do so. But in fact it is disastrous, for it obscures thought and confuses language.

Thus there is no doubt as to the general resemblance of the Christian offer of salvation to that of other cults, and the obvious point of difference—the presence of the Jewish eschatology—has no claim to superior truth. What, then, are the points of difference between Christianity and the other cults which explain the triumph of the Church? Two popular but probably mistaken explanations may first be discussed.

It is often said that Christianity had an enormous advantage in that Jesus was an historic person, whereas the Lords of the other cults were not. But closer analysis does not confirm the importance of this difference.

The initiates of the other cults believed that their Lords were historic persons, just as Christians believed that Jesus was. They had, indeed, lived a long time ago, but this was no disadvantage: any one who reads Tatian's *Oratio ad Graecos* can see how antiquity, not recentness, was regarded as desirable. The general argument of Christians was not that Jesus was historic, and the other Lords were not, but that he fulfilled a true offer of salvation, made in a more remote antiquity than any pagan religion could claim, while the heathen Lords were demons, misunderstanding the prophecies of the Old Testament, clumsily simulating their fulfilment, and arrogating to themselves the title of God. It was of course an advantage that the "sacred legend" of Christianity was free from the repulsive elements in other cults, which it taxed the ingenuity of a Julian to explain.

Moreover, historical criticism shows that the points in the story of Jesus which played the greatest part in commending Christianity to a generation asking for private salvation are those which are not historic. The element of truth in much perverse criticism, arguing that Jesus never existed, is that the Jesus of history is quite different from the Lord assumed as the founder of Catholic Christianity. The Church conquered the world by offering salvation through a redeeming Lord. Jesus made no such offer: to him the Kingdom of God, the pearl of great price, was the natural inheritance of men, if they would only take it. No supernatural change of nature, but to turn round, abandon all that hindered, and go in the right direction—go home—was the repentance which he required. Probably it was not unique teaching: it is very hard to obey, and it makes no spectacular demands. Its only claim to acceptance is its truth. It did not conquer the world. Nor did Jesus—the Jesus of history—think that it would do so. "Strait is the gate and narrow is the way that leadeth unto Life, and few there are that find it."

Thus the theory that Catholic Christianity succeeded because Jesus was an historic person cannot be sustained.

Nor is there much more truth in the attribution of its success to the influence of the personality of Jesus. No doubt it was the personality of Jesus which influenced his immediate followers, made them regard him as the Davidic Messiah or as "Son of Man," and rendered possible their belief in his exaltation to the right hand of God. Without this belief Christianity could never have come into existence; but once the belief was established it became the foundation of the whole structure, and the personality of Jesus was quite eclipsed by the supernatural value attached to him. Not the men who had known Jesus, but those who had not, converted the Roman Empire, and their gospel was that of the Cross, Resurrection, and Parousia, not the Sermon on the Mount, or an ethical interpretation of the Parables, or a moral *imitatio Christi*.

The true answer is that Catholic Christianity conquered because it was popular, not because it was true, and failed for the same reason. Permanence, not popularity, is the test of truth; for truth has often no adherents, while error has many.

The permanent truth in Christianity is, I think, to be found in the spirit, or perhaps more correctly the "will," which Jesus had, and tried to hand on to his disciples, of service and self-sacrifice. It calls men to redeem others, rather than to seek redemption for themselves. This is to spiritual life what gravitation is to the physical world. It was known to others before him and after, but it has not yet conquered the world.

But the popular teaching [1] which loomed largest in the early days of the Church offered the privilege rather than the responsibility of redemption, and maintained that the Christian was united to the Supreme God—a claim higher than that made by any other cult. This side of Christianity, though not Jewish, was in the main derived from Judaism, from which all the first Christian missionaries accepted the preaching of the one supreme God, whom Paul constantly refers to as "the Father." There has been of recent years much loose writing and looser speech about the "Fatherhood of God." It has even been asserted that this was the special revelation of Jesus. Such a view does not for a moment sustain any critical inves-

[1] I would emphasise the word popular. The great missionaries were doubtless inspired by the desire to save others, by the will to minister rather than be ministered to, and by a readiness to give their lives as a ransom for others, but their converts were otherwise minded.

tigation. No doubt Jesus sometimes, possibly often, spoke of God as "Father"; but so did many other Jews. They and he referred to the moral sonship of the righteous, not to a supernatural or sacramental relation. Nor is there any sign that Jesus felt that he had any new revelation as to the nature of God: he was much more intent on telling men what they ought to do to conform to the demands of God.

But after the time of Jesus the use of "Father" as applied to God became more and more general; especially to denote the peculiar relationship—however that may have been conceived—between Jesus and God. This use is especially characteristic of the editor of Matthew, and still more of the Fourth Gospel. It is the correlative to the process by which "Jesus, the Son of God," became "God the Son."

The Hellenistic Christians seem to have been particularly fond of this use; partly perhaps from linguistic reasons. The Greek for Jehovah is κύριος, Lord; but this word had been already taken as the title of Jesus. Therefore when a Christian-speaking Greek wished to refer to Jehovah he could not without ambiguity say "The Lord," and he began to adopt the usage of referring to Jehovah as "the Father." But what would have been the implication to Greek ears of this usage? Two lines were possible: it could be interpreted as referring exclusively to the relation between God and Jesus, or as referring to the relation between God and men. Paul is evidence that the second, as well as the first, was accepted. "As many as are led by the Spirit of God, they are Sons of God." But how would a Greek have understood this verse? Probably he would have thought that it meant that the gift of the Spirit changed men's nature; so that, as Irenaeus said, two generations later, they were no longer mortal men but the children of the immortal God. To the Greek the gift of the Spirit was the gift of divine nature, immortal and incorruptible. That is, of course,

in nowise Jewish: even if Paul meant this, which is
doubtful, he did so by virtue of his Greek associations.
The question, however, has not been adequately discussed
how far this interpretation is exactly the same as that of
the other cults. It clearly brought the Christian into
direct relation with the Supreme God, through the Lord.
Was this so in Mithraism or in the cult of Isis? In both
of them it seems rather that the initiate was brought
rather into relationship with the Lord.[1] Surely it was a
real advantage to Christian propaganda that the Church
offered union with the Supreme God more definitely than
did any rival cult.

Two elements must be distinguished in such teaching.
Permanently important in it is the recognition of the fact
that a helping hand of grace stretches out from the unknown to help man when he cries from the depths: but
it contains also a theory as to the origin and nature of
grace. The fact is indisputable, the theory depends on
evidence; and there is really none to justify confident
assertion. No doubt it was an enormous asset to Christianity to proclaim that the grace found by its adherents
came straight from the cause of all existence. The same
situation was reproduced after the Reformation, and it

---

[1] This statement would be required to be modified for detailed
application to various classes both among Christians and among
initiates in the other cults. In all cults there was probably an
uneducated substratum which thought very little about the subject.
It was satisfied with the fact of salvation, and was not specially
interested in its method. On the other hand, the educated with a
metaphysical tendency were interested in the relation of the Lord
of the cult to the Supreme God, and this might, in time, have
produced something similar to the Christological speculations of the
fourth century. Apuleius seems to identify the Supreme God with
the Lord in a manner which at times reminds the reader of Sabellian Christianity. On the other hand, Heliogabalus seems to have
produced a complete amalgam between Mithras and Helios, and reminds us of the tendency of uneducated Christianity in all generations to make the gospel become the preaching of the new God,
or the true God, Jesus, of which I heard a somewhat extreme
example from a preacher who maintained fervidly that Jehovah was
the Hebrew of Jesus.

was an asset to Protestantism to claim direct access to God, without the mediation of saints. Nevertheless, it is hard to see that there is any evidence to favour the theory that grace comes in the one way rather than the other. The element of truth in the early Christian teaching is not the side which was most popular, but rather that which, a little later, partly unconsciously, animated the Church in rejecting Marcionism—the conviction that there is no essential disharmony or final clash in history, that the God of creation is not hostile to the God of grace.[1]

Moreover, it was not only—or even chiefly—the helping hand of grace in the troubles and sorrows of life which Greek Christians especially hoped for by union with the supreme God or by the power of Jesus. It was rather the gift of eternal Life after death, which was the special characteristic of the Gods. The points of importance are the means whereby they thought that this immortality was obtained, and the nature which they ascribed to it.

The act by which the faithful acquired immortality was Baptism. The history of this distinctively Christian rite is obscure. From the standpoint of the historian of religions it is the combination of a Jewish ceremony with Graeco-Oriental ideas. The Jews had frequently practised ceremonial washing with a religious significance—generally speaking, purification from the guilt of offences against the ritual law; it was also part of the initiation of proselytes, and had been largely practised by John the Forerunner. But in no case did any Jew think that washing could change, sacramentally or magically, the nature of man. A Greek on the other hand, brought up in the atmosphere of the mysteries, might well have thought so. The same is true of the other constituent

---

[1] See the last chapter of F. C. Burkitt's *The Gospel History and its Transmission*. This chapter is a most clear-sighted analysis of one of the essentials of Catholic truth as opposed to error, and I venture to say this because its importance seems in general to be overlooked.

element in primitive Christian Baptism—the formula "in the name of the Lord Jesus." There is no reason why Jews should not have used the name of Jesus for magical purposes—indeed they undoubtedly did so—for magic was not peculiar to the Greeks. But the ordinary Jew would never have practised magic to secure immortality or to become divine. He believed that immortality was the natural lot of all the chosen people who kept the Law, and would be reached, not through sacraments or secret knowledge, but through the resurrection at the last day. Thus it is possible that the first Jewish Christians may have practised baptism by an extension of the ordinary ritual of proselyte-making, or as a means of securing remission of sins, in the spirit of John the Baptist, but it is extremely improbable that it was for them the sacrament of regeneration to eternal life which it was held to be by Greek Christians.

Turning from the possibilities and probabilities suggested by the history of religion to the evidence of the early literature critically studied, two points stand out as probable. First, Jesus neither practised nor enjoined baptism of any kind; secondly, the Antiochean missionaries always practised baptism "in the name of the Lord Jesus." The second point is so obviously proved both by Acts and the Pauline epistles that it requires no discussion. The first has the limitations of the argument from silence, for it rests on the fact that there is no trace of Baptism by Jesus, either by practice or precept, in the synoptic gospels, except a single statement in Matt. xxviii. 19, in which the risen Jesus is represented as commanding the disciples to undertake the conversion of the Gentiles ($\tau \grave{a}$ $\check{\epsilon}\theta\nu\eta$) and their baptism in the name of the Father, Son, and Holy Spirit. That this verse is not historical but a late tradition, intended to support ecclesiastical practice, is shown by the absence of the trine formula of baptism in Acts and the Epistles, and the extreme reluctance with which the apostles, who are sup-

mortality of the soul was preserved by the tradition of the Mysteries,[1] not by the Academy.

Stoics and Epicureans, far more important for the first century than Academics, were materialists; but that does not mean that they did not believe in the existence of a human soul or spirit. Spirit was for them merely the most attenuated form of matter. The spirit of man might be dissipated after death, as the grosser material composing his body would be, or it might survive and retain consciousness and memory until the cycle came round when all things, including human careers, would be repeated.

But the first Greek Christians were scarcely influenced by an intelligent comprehension of Stoic metaphysics, and attempts made to trace their direct influence in Paul or elsewhere only show that their vocabulary was more widely used than their problems were understood—a phenomenon not peculiar to the first century. All that can be said with any confidence is that the expectation of blessed immortality—not for all but for the chosen few—fostered by the mysteries was probably most often conceived as the survival of the soul after death, and the soul in turn was conceived as "Spirit," a highly attenuated material existence, which was found until death in the body, and was then released from it.

In some such way the Greeks in Corinth who were converted to Christianity expected immortality. So they did also in the other cults offering salvation. The points of difference in Christianity are in the kind of life which was demanded from initiates, and in the final consummation expected.

1 Corinthians shows clearly that some Hellenic Christians held that having secured immortality they were free

---

[1] From which indeed Plato had probably obtained it. He justified it, handily enough, from his doctrine of Ideas, but scarcely derived it thence. The triumph of Aristotle destroyed his justification, but the parent stream flowed on placidly, undisturbed by thought.

to do as they liked with their bodies. Paul insisted on the observance of that morality which was central in Judaism. He had rendered his task difficult by his rejection of the Law, but he won his fight, and the permanent association of Jewish morality with the Christian Church and its Hellenic Christology and sacraments was the result.

In the same way Paul contended successfully for the Jewish doctrine of a resurrection, though with some modifications. This was not the same thing as the Greek belief in personal immortality. The Sadducees, indeed, may have Hellenised on this subject, as did some of the Alexandrian Jews, represented by the Wisdom of Solomon. But the bulk of the people followed the Pharisees and looked for a resurrection of the body, at the end of the age.

Paul and the other missionaries continued to teach this Jewish doctrine, but were not at once able to convince their Greek hearers that immortality must necessarily be reached through a resurrection of the body. Presumably the Greeks felt that immortality was sufficient, and a future reunion between an immortal soul and a resuscitated body was as undesirable as improbable. Paul in 1 Corinthians insists on the Jewish doctrine, but he makes the concession to the Greeks that the resurrection will not be of flesh and blood but of a "spiritual" body, that is to say, a body consisting of the most attenuated form of matter. It will be the same body, but it will be changed.

This modified form of Jewish thought was supported by an appeal to the case of Jesus, who had already risen from the dead. The appeal was really far more effective than the rest of Paul's argument, which was not calculated to convince the doubtful, and it has the special importance for the historian that it proves that Paul did not think the risen Jesus had a body of flesh and blood, and believed that in this he was in agreement with all the early witnesses.

Nevertheless, the belief of the Church soon affirmed what remained its unchanged faith until the nineteenth century—the resurrection of the flesh, both of the Lord in the past, and of the Christian in the future. This was the triumph of Jewish thought, and is an exception to the general rule that Christianity became steadily more Hellenic.

The reason why Jewish thought triumphed is difficult to ascertain. Few hypotheses as to a future life have less intrinsic probability than that ultimately reached, which postulates an immortal soul living discarnate until the resurrection day, when it will be reunited to its own resuscitated body, and both will be rewarded or punished by the final judgement of God. Nevertheless this hypothesis supplanted all others.

Two causes may be suggested. The pressure of the Docetic controversy, which insisted that Jesus had never been a real man of flesh and blood, but a spirit appearing in human form, made the Church attach greater weight to the reality of his flesh and blood, even after the resurrection. Hence arose the narratives of the appearances of the risen Jesus in Luke and John, emphasising this point. That they there are secondary seems to be proved by the evidence of 1 Cor. xv. Hence, too, it may be, came the suppression of the missing end of Mark. Following this tendency it was natural to argue, as Paul had done, that Christians like Jesus would be raised with the same bodies which they had had.

A different motive was provided by moral considerations. It is clear that there was danger, even in the Corinth of Paul's days, of men arguing that, having obtained the Spirit and consequent immortality, nothing carnal had any importance: the body had, as it were, but a short time, and might be allowed to enjoy itself as it chose. To combat this danger of an absolutely licentious position the Church maintained that the body was as

eternal as the soul, and that its future happiness depended
on its present behaviour.

Both these factors undoubtedly entered into the development of Christian thought; and they were reinforced
by the natural desire of man to preserve the pleasures of
life in a body of flesh and blood.

The whole question of the expectation of immortality
is as obscure as it is interesting.   Direct evidence in
favour of a survival of individual consciousness after
death is provided in the present by psychical research,
and from the past by narratives of the apparitions of the
dead, among which the story of the appearances of the
risen Jesus must be classed.   To most minds the evidence
does not justify a decisive verdict of any nature.

The "moral" argument is equally evasive.   To certain
minds in certain moods it seems incredible that extinction
can await beings who display the qualities manifested by
men at their best, animated by such high purposes, so
little fulfilled.   In Christian circles the argument has
helped to secure the orthodox belief in the resurrection of
the body.   But, on the other hand, this belief has received
a succession of shocks from other considerations.   The
resuscitation of the flesh has become more and more incredible.   Bishop Westcott endeavoured to meet this feeling by reviving the Pauline notion of a body of "Spirit,"
and was followed by Bishop Gore in so doing.   The
process was helped by the fact that in the English creed
resurrectio carnis is translated *resurrection of the body,*
so that the denial of the Apostles' Creed involved in the
Westcott-Gore interpretation could be softened into an
apparent affirmation.

Even more serious, though less often expressed, is the
moral objection to the judgement, which dooms men to
extremes of bliss or misery in accordance as they fall one
side or the other of a certain line.   The conscience of the

modern man feels that no one deserves either Heaven or
Hell. Moreover, this same conscience doubts whether any
one really deserves complete perpetuation. All men are
of mixed nature; some elements seem to deserve to be
eliminated, and others to survive. Thus the moral indict-
ment against the old expectation of judgement is that no
one deserves either of its extremes.

A just judgement would be not between man and man,
saving one and condemning the other, but between different parts of each of us. For in man good and evil
are always present: what we ask for is not complete survival, but the ultimate elimination of some parts and the
constant growth of others; we desire change, not permanence.[1] Moreover, even in the short space of life which
we can observe, elimination and selection are clearly
present. The child and the old man are one, not by
identity but by continuity of life. The main object of
education is to further and confirm this beneficent change.
Once more, this, or something like it, is often put forward as the meaning of the doctrine of "judgement."
But when the creed states that Jesus will "come again in
glory to judge both the quick and dead," it means the
Jewish eschatological expectation, and to use its language
to express modern thought is unfair to both.

All such thoughts are *a priori*, and can never convince
the reluctant. The path of wisdom is not to weigh the
merits of various inconclusive arguments, but to distinguish between Desire and Knowledge.

Desire for most men is to remain essentially as they
are. The healthy enjoy life, and even the unhealthy cling
to it. If we are candid most of us admit that we should
like indefinitely prolonged existence, that we have an
infinite curiosity to know what is going to happen in the
world, and a wish to take part in its development. That
is Desire.

[1] This has much in common with Origen's teaching, but unfortunately Origen was rejected by the Catholic Church.

Over against Desire is Knowledge. We know that matter is indestructible, though it changes its form, and that energy is equally indestructible, but constantly varies its form. If Life be similar to energy this gives us reason to believe that it is permanent, but that its form changes. If, however, Life be a form of Energy, not a force similar to it, there is no reason to expect its permanence. The chief reason against this view is that whereas we can convert heat into electricity, or electricity into light, we cannot—as yet—convert either into Life.

So far Knowledge takes us on the hypothesis that Life is material, for Energy is not outside of the world of matter. But still within the field of Knowledge is the old problem of Immaterial Reality and its relation to Life. To those who are convinced, as I am myself, by the old arguments in favour of Immaterial Reality, conceivable but not imaginable, it is certain that intellectual and moral life belongs to it and shares its attributes of eternity. Metaphysics are more convincing than psychology. But need this mean that this eternal life is personal? No one as yet has answered this question.

And there are further considerations: all that we know of life teaches us that it is a succession of losses. The passage from youth to middle life, and the change from middle life to old age are losses, from which we shrink. No man willingly surrenders the flexibility of youth or the power of middle life. But the experience—shrunk from and postponed though it be—teaches that through loss came gain. Yet none of us ever foresaw the form which the gain would take. After old age comes death: that too is loss. Is it also gain? If Life continue, and that at least seems probable, Knowledge teaches us that it will change its form and that here, too, gain will come through loss. But, it is often said, this is the denial of the survival of personality, and it is personality, not life, which we desire. No doubt we do: but we desire to keep much which we lose, and yet come to see that only thus could we achieve the greater gain.[1]

After all, Faith is not belief in spite of evidence, but life in scorn of consequence—a courageous trust in the great purpose of all things and pressing forward to finish the work which is in sight, whatever the price may be. Who knows whether the "personality" of which men talk so much and know so little may not prove to be the temporary limitation rather than the necessary expression of Life?

There was once an archipelago of islands off a mountainous coast separated from each other and from the mainland by the sea. But in course of time the sea dried up, the islands were joined to the great mountain behind them, and it became clear that they had always been united by solid ground under a very shallow sea. If those islands could have thought and spoken what would they have said? Before the event they would have protested against losing their insularity, but would they have done so afterwards, when the water which divided them from each other was gone, and they knew that they were part of the great mountain which before they had only dimly seen, obscured by the mists rising from the sea?

[1] See additional note on p. 107.

V

ROME AND EPHESUS

CORINTH as portrayed in the Epistles of Paul
gives us our simplest and least contaminated picture of the Hellenic Christianity which regarded
itself as the cult of the Lord Jesus, who offered salvation
—immortality—to those initiated in his mysteries. It
had obvious weaknesses in the eyes of Jewish Christians,
even when they were as Hellenised as Paul, since it offered
little reason for a higher standard of conduct than heathenism, and its personal eschatology left no real place for
the resurrection of the body. The Epistles of Paul to the
Corinthians are in the main protests against this Hellenic
weakness, and the real monument to Paul in the first two,
or perhaps even four, centuries is the success which he had
in driving home these protests. Owing to later controversies we are apt to treat Justification by Faith as Paul's
greatest contribution to the Church. Possibly that is
true, if the whole of Church history be taken into account,
but the attempt to reconstruct "Paulinism" on this principle produces the result that the effect of Paul's teaching
cannot be traced in any of the Christian writings of the
next two centuries. This is obviously absurd: if Paul's
writings were preserved so carefully his teaching on some
great points must have been regarded as central. Nor,
if we succeed in forgetting the emphasis introduced by
later controversies, is it hard to see what these points
were. As against the Jews, Paul, the Greek, insisted on
Freedom from the Law. That stood. As against the
Greek, Paul insisted on Jewish morality and on the Res-

urrection of the body. These also stood. And these three points, if we may judge from subapostolic writings, were those which influenced the Church most. No doubt Paul preached Jesus as the crucified but risen and glorified Lord, and no doubt regarded Baptism and the Eucharist as sacraments, but so did all Hellenic Christians. Probably he would have regarded his doctrine of Faith and Justification as of primary importance, but all the existing evidence seems to show that it failed to convince the Jews, or to be remembered by the Gentiles, until it was rediscovered by Augustine.

Sacramental Christianity with an emphasis on morality was henceforward the true characteristic of the Church. But it had yet to give a more detailed account of the Lord, and to attempt to come to terms with Greek philosophy.

Except with regard to the Second Coming, the Jewish ideas of the Davidic Messiah and of the Son of Man ceased to have any living importance. It was not doubted that the Lord was divine, but there were two ways of considering his divinity. One was to regard Jesus as a man who had been inspired by the Holy Spirit, and had himself been taken up into the sphere of divinity after his death, so that he, as well as the spirit which had been in him, was now divine. This form of thought is generally known as Adoptionism. The other way was to think of Jesus as a pre-existent divine being who had become human.

The difference between the two forms of thought is that whereas Adoptionism postulates a distinct human personality for the human Jesus, which had a beginning in time and was promoted to divinity, the other theory postulates only a divine person who became human. Both theories, therefore, begin with much the same doctrine of God, as consisting, if the metaphor may be used, of the two factors of the Father and the Spirit, who was sometimes called his Son,[1] and was frequently identified with the Logos of the Greek philosophers. There is very little evidence in early Christian writings for that distinction between the Logos and the Spirit which afterward became orthodox.

The competing existence of Adoptionist and Pre-existent Christology does much to explain the early development of the doctrine of the Trinity. Starting with the Father and the Spirit-son, Adoptionism added a third to the sphere of divinity, namely, the glorified Jesus. This belief was preserved in the baptismal formula of the Church of Rome, as found in Justin Martyr, which was "In the name of the Father of all, and in the name of Jesus Christ who was crucified under Pontius Pilate, and in the name of the Holy Spirit," and though Adoptionism was in the end rejected, it left its permanent mark on Christian theology in the "threeness"[2] of the doctrine of God. The doctrines of Pre-existent Christology could scarcely have had this result,[3] for it is quite clear that the Logos and the Spirit were distinguished only in language, and the Incarnation was, as it were, but an incident in the work of the Logos.

Few things are more needed than study of this side of the growth of Christian doctrine. Harnack's *History of Doctrine* has indeed done something, but many of the details of his work require to be worked out, and some of his statements need revision.[4] Older books, such as Dorner's *History of the Doctrine of the Person of Christ,*

[1] This proves that this form of thought is not Semitic; had it been so, the Spirit would scarcely have been masculine.

[2] It would be unfair and misleading to say the doctrine of the Trinity. That doctrine is not the statement of the "threeness" of God, but of the relation which this bears to his unity.

[3] No doubt the "threeness" was emphasized by the habit of three immersions in baptism, whatever the origin of this practice may be, and by philosophic reflections as to the properties of triangles such as are found in Philo.

[4] Illuminating suggestions can be found in F. C. Conybeare's *The Key of Truth* and in H. Usener's *Weihnachtsfest.*

admirable though they are, have little value for this purpose, for they were written chiefly with the object of explaining and leading up to Nicene and Chalcedonian doctrine. All that can be done in these pages is to indicate certain lines, which might be profitably followed up, as to the two chief centres of development, Rome and Ephesus, the former representing in the main Adoptionism and the latter Pre-existent Christology.

After Antioch Rome seems to have been the most important centre of Christianity in the first and early second centuries. Certainly it was more important than Corinth, though in some ways, owing to the preservation of Paul's correspondence, we know more about Corinth than Rome. Fortunately there are extant a number of documents which illustrate its history, though none of them throw any real light on its foundation, for it is unknown who was the founder of the Church in Rome.

The first of these documents is Paul's Epistle to the Romans, but it is very strange how little this tells us as to the history or nature of the Church in that city. Apparently Paul was acquainted with Christians in Rome before he went there himself, but there is no suggestion that he regarded the Church there as the foundation of Peter or of any other of the leading missionaries. It is therefore by no means impossible that the Church of Rome sprang up by the coming to the city in increasing numbers of men who had been converted elsewhere. Whether the Epistle to the Romans was originally intended for that city or not is an open question,[1] but at least it was sent to Rome in one of its forms, and that is after all the most

---

[1] In the *Earlier Epistles of St. Paul*, pp. 335 ff. (especially p. 368), I suggested that the shorter recension of the Epistle to the Romans, the existence of which is proved by the evidence of the Latin *breves*, Tertullian, Cyprian, and Marcion, and by the textual confusion surrounding the final doxology, may be the same as that which omits all mention of Rome, and that, if so, it was probably written originally for some other destination. This suggestion has met with little approbation from critics, but with even less discussion. I still think that it is worth consideration.

important fact. The most remarkable thing about the
revelation which it makes of the Christianity at Rome is
that the problems which seem to have interested or dis-
tracted the Church are so much more Jewish than Hellenic.
The questions of the Law and of the ultimate fate of
Israel are so extensively dealt with as to suggest a strongly
Jewish element in the Church. Jesus is, as in Corinth,
a Redeemer, but the problems of life for those who
accepted him suggest Jewish rather than Greek ante-
cedents.

What is the bearing of Romans on the Christology of
the Church at Rome? Not, that is to say, what is its
evidence as to the thought of Paul, but how are certain
phrases in it likely to have been interpreted? The most
important passage is Romans i. 1-4: "Paul, a servant of
Jesus Christ, a called apostle, separated to God's gospel
which He had promised beforehand by His prophets in
Holy Scriptures concerning His Son, who became of the
seed of David according to the flesh, who was appointed
Son of God miraculously according to the spirit of holiness by resurrection from the dead, Jesus Christ our
Lord." [1]   What is this likely to have meant to those who
read it in Greek without any knowledge of a "Pre-
existent" Christology? I think that they would have been
impressed by the parallelisms in the sentence: κατὰ σάρκα
is parallel to κατὰ πνεῦμα ἀγιωσύνης and ἐκ σπέρματος Δαυείδ
is parallel to ἐξ ἀναστάσεως νεκρῶν. It would thus mean that
Jesus had been a human being by belonging to the family
of David, and had been ordained, or appointed to be a
"Spirit of holiness," by being raised from the dead:
κατὰ σάρκα explains the result of γενομένου ἐκ σπέρματος
Δαυείδ, and κατὰ πνεῦμα ἀγιωσύνης explains the result of
ὁρισθέντος υἱοῦ . . . ἐξ ἀναστάσεως νεκρῶν. That is Adop-

---

[1] Παῦλος δοῦλος Ἰησοῦ Χριστοῦ κλητὸς ἀπόστολος ἀφωρισμένος εἰς εὐαγγέλιον
θεοῦ ὃ προεπηγγείλατο διὰ τῶν προφητῶν αὐτοῦ ἐν γραφαῖς ἀγίαις περὶ τοῦ υἱοῦ
αὐτοῦ τοῦ γενομένου ἐκ σπέρματος Δαυείδ κατὰ σάρκα τοῦ ὁρισθέντος υἱοῦ θεοῦ ἐν
δυνάμει κατὰ πνεῦμα ἀγιωσύνης ἐξ ἀναστάσεως νεκρῶν Ἰησοῦ Χριστοῦ τοῦ κυρίου
ἡμῶν.

tionism, and though the passage has been explained in terms of a pre-existent Christology by those who for other reasons are convinced that this was the real nature of Paul's doctrine, it could be taken quite easily in this Adoptionist way, for ὁρισθέντος could mean "became by means of appointment" quite as well as ἀφωρισμένος could mean the same thing with regard to Paul's apostleship.[1] The general impression made by the verse would be, to any one who had Adoptionist views already, that Jesus, who was born as a human being into the family of David (which gave him a certain well-understood claim to the title Son of God), had by the Resurrection been promoted to another kind of sonship, not as a human being of flesh, but as a spiritual being.

The next document in probable chronological order which seems to belong to Rome is the Epistle to the Hebrews. It is much disputed by critics whether it was written in Rome or to Rome, but that it was extant there can hardly be doubted in view of the extensive quotations from it in the Epistle of Clement. It reveals a different mind from that of the Epistle to the Romans, but once more it is Jewish questions which are uppermost. The main problem is the meaning of the ritual law. Nevertheless, as in Romans, there are sufficient traces of sacramental teaching to make it clear that Christianity in Rome as in Corinth meant the sacramental cult of a saving Lord. This was the basis of everything, but the problems which arose from the attempt to work out its implications are as markedly Jewish in Rome as they are Greek in Corinth. It does not mean, of course, that there were no Greeks in Rome, any more than that there were no Jews in Corinth, but the dominating influence was Jewish in one and Greek in the other.

---

[1] The justification for assuming that the Church at Rome probably had Adoptionist proclivities is the undeniable fact that early in the second century Hermas held this view, and there is no evidence that he was an innovator.

The Epistle to the Hebrews seems at first to be much more obviously "Pre-existent" in its Christology than the Epistle to the Romans, indeed it could well be explained on the theory that it was maintaining a Pre-existent Christology against a rival form of the same general type which identified the pre-existent Christ with an angel. But if one ask whether this would have been clear to a reader with Adoptionist principles, it can be seen that he would very easily have interpreted it in accordance with his own ideas. The question of what the Son of God was before the Incarnation is not the centre of the discussion. What is important is the function of High Priest in Heaven which he now fulfils, and this function is the consequence of his human life. It is true that in the first chapter there are phrases which are most naturally explained by "pre-existent" doctrine, but though the writer appears to be explaining the essential superiority of the Son to angels, in chapter ii. this superiority is the result of the Passion and Resurrection, and in verse 10 the divine being, "through whom and for whom are all things," is distinguished from the leader of our salvation, who is, of course, Jesus.[1] It is plain that this verse, difficult to understand on other lines of thought, is quite intelligible if it be interpreted in the light of that Adoptionism which, as we know from Hermas, used "Son of God" for the Holy Spirit and also for the glorified Jesus.

It is very hard not to discuss this question as though Adoptionism and Pre-existent Christology were consciously competing systems from the beginning. That is of course not true: none of these writers was consciously discussing the question. For this reason elements can be

---

[1] Ἔπρεπεν γὰρ αὐτῷ δι' ὃν τὰ πάντα καὶ δι' οὗ τὰ πάντα πολλοὺς υἱοὺς εἰς δόξαν ἀγαγόντα τὸν ἀρχηγὸν τῆς σωτηρίας αὐτῶν διὰ παθημάτων τελειῶσαι. The English translators take ἀγαγόντα as referring to the same person as αὐτῷ, but it seems grammatically preferable to construe it as a qualification of ἀρχηγόν.

found in the Epistle to the Romans and in the Epistle to the Hebrews which are easily susceptible of an Adoptionist interpretation, and others equally indicative of Preexistent Christology. This means that Christians at that moment had not formulated the problem. But *The Shepherd* of Hermas shows that in Rome an important body of Christians did become wholly Adoptionist, and if they used Romans and Hebrews, they probably interpreted the passages indicated above in agreement with their own opinions and passed over the rest—in accordance with the best tradition of Biblical commentators.

A third document is the first Epistle of Peter. If this were really written by Peter it cannot be much later in date than Romans, and would probably be earlier than Hebrews, but it seems increasingly clear that the Epistle refers to a later period, and cannot be the work of the Apostle. It is concerned in the main with the problem of persecution, and though the matter is extremely obscure, on the whole a date early in the second century in the time of Trajan and Pliny seems the most likely. Whether the indications that it comes from Rome are not part of the fiction of its authorship is at least open to question, but the point is not very important. If it be really Roman it shows traces of a further development of sacramental Christianity, but does not throw much light on its details. It has some similarity in language to Romans, but very little in the picture presented of Christianity. The central point in it is the emphasis on baptismal regeneration, which gives Christians the certainty of immortality. The eschatological expectation of the "revelation of Jesus Christ" is strongly marked, but there is no emphasis on the hope of resurrection. On one point, however, there is a close resemblance to Paul. Spirit and flesh are contrasted, and it is clearly implied that after death the Christian, like the Christ, is spirit and not flesh. It throws little light on the question of Adoptionism, for though there is nothing in it which contradicts Pre-exist-

ent Christology, there is also nothing in it which would
have startled an Adoptionist.

After this [1] comes the first Epistle of Clement, a letter
sent by the Church of Rome to the Church at Corinth.
It is generally dated at the end of the first century, but
there is really very little evidence, and it is curious that
this date should be accepted with so little hesitation by
almost all critics. It is in the main an ethical treatise,
more especially on the importance of good order in the
community. This teaching is based almost exclusively on
the Old Testament.

There is very little in 1 Clement which throws any
light on Christology or on sacraments. For the history
of doctrine, in fact, 1 Clement is, considering its length,
a remarkably disappointing document, but two passages
are important. In 1 Clement xlii., "The Apostles received
the Gospel for us from the Lord Jesus Christ, Jesus the
Christ was sent from God," there is a clear statement of
the supernatural claims of the apostles, but made in such
a way as to imply a lower view of Christ than Nicene
orthodoxy: he is the middle term between God and the
apostles, and is separated from the one as clearly as from
the other. The "Lord" is more than man, but is not God.
The excellence of the Lord is also expressed in 1 Clement
xxxvi., in words reminiscent of Hebrews. "This is the
way" (*i.e.* the way referred to in Psalms l. 23, "The
sacrifice of praise shall glorify me, and therein is a way
in which I will show him the salvation of God") "beloved,
in which we found our salvation, Jesus Christ, the high
priest of our offerings, the defender and helper of our

---

[1] Though, if the late date for 1 Peter be accepted, 1 Clement is the
earlier document. But the chronology of 1 Clement seems to me
less certain than it is usually held to be. It depends on two factors,
both doubtful: (1) the chronology of the list of Roman bishops
in Eusebius and in the *Liber Pontificalis;* (2) the supposed reference in the epistle to the alleged persecution under Domitian.
Against these is the reference to Clement in *The Shepherd* of
Hermas, and the apparently clear testimony of the Canon of Mura-
tori that *The Shepherd* was written about A.D. 140.

weakness. Through him we fix our gaze on the heights of heaven, through him we see the reflection of his fault-less and lofty countenance, through him the eyes of our hearts were opened, through him our foolish and darkened understanding blossoms toward the light, through him the Master (*i.e.* God) willed that we should taste the immortal knowledge, 'who being the brightness of his majesty is by so much greater than angels, as he hath inherited a more excellent name.' For it is written that 'Who maketh his angels spirits, and his ministers a flame of fire.' But of his son the Master said thus, 'Thou art my Son, to-day have I begotten thee; ask of me and I will give thee the heathen for thine inheritance.' " The resemblance to Hebrews is obvious, but throws less light than might be expected on Clement's Christology. What did he think was the meaning of "To-day have I begotten thee"? The one point which comes out clearly is that the Church was regarded as an institution for the securing of the salva-tion offered by the death of Christ. It has a divine authority, for just as Christ came from God, so the Apostles came from Christ. It may almost be said that the Epistle has a high Ecclesiology but an undeveloped Christology.

Thus the Christianity revealed by 1 Clement suggests a Church which had accepted Jewish ethics and a Jewish hope for resurrection, and regarded Jesus as the divine messenger of God, who in turn had appointed the Apostles as the foundation of the Church. It is a very simple form of cult, and in the prayer which Clement quotes almost everything is directed towards the Father. It is Hellen-ised Judaism without the ceremonial law, but with a be-lief in Jesus and the Church.

The next document concerned with the Church of Rome is in many ways the most important. *The Shepherd* of Hermas is not an easy book to appreciate at first. It is a series of interviews between Hermas and various supernatural beings who give him good advice. It may be as late as 140, but many think that it is earlier. The book was written with the practical purpose of guiding rightly the Christians in Rome. There is nothing in Hermas which really contradicts anything in 1 Clement, but it supplements it in several directions. In the first place, like Clement, it attaches great importance to the Church. No salvation is possible except in the Church, and those who are and remain in it secure eternal life, or, in the phrase of Hermas himself, "live to God." The only point on which Hermas is really different is that he seems to have nothing to say about a resurrection, and apparently was content with immortality. But this may be merely an accident and cannot be pressed.

The book throws great light on the development of thought and practice in Rome, and its Christology is the most instructive example which we possess of early Adoptionism.

The evidence is so important, and Hermas is in general so little studied, that the main passage (Sim. v. 2. 1 ff.) may be quoted: "Listen to the Parable which I am going to tell you concerning Fasting. A certain man had a field, and many servants, and on part of the field he planted a vineyard. And he chose out a certain servant, who was faithful, in good esteem and honour with him, and he called him and said to him: Take this vineyard which I have planted, and fence it until I come, and do nothing more to the vineyard. And follow this order of mine and you shall have your freedom from me. And the master of the servant went abroad. Now when he had gone the servant took and fenced the vineyard, and when he had finished the fencing of the vineyard he saw that the vineyard was full of weeds. Therefore he reasoned in himself, saying: I have finished this order of the Lord; I will next dig this vineyard, and it will be better when it is dug, and having no weeds will yield more fruit, not being choked by the weeds. He took and dug the vineyard, and pulled out all the weeds which were in the

vineyard. And that vineyard became very beautiful and
fertile with no weeds to choke it. After a time the master
of the servant and the field came, and entered into the
vineyard, and seeing the vineyard beautifully fenced, and
moreover, dug, and all the weeds pulled up and vines
fertile, he was greatly pleased at the acts of the servant.
So he called his beloved son, whom he had as heir, and
his friends whom he had as counsellors, and told them
what he had ordered his servant, and what he had found
accomplished. And they congratulated the servant on
the character which the master gave him. And he said
to them: 'I promised this servant his freedom if he kept
the orders which I gave him. Now he has kept my orders,
and has added good work in the vineyard, and greatly
pleased me. So in reward for this work which he has
done I wish to make him joint-heir with my son, because,
when he had a good thought he did not put it on one side,
but carried it out. The son of the master agreed with
this plan, that the servant should be joint-heir with the
son. After a few days he made a feast and sent to him
much food from the feast. But the servant took the food
which was sent to him by the master, kept what was
sufficient for himself, and distributed the rest to his fellow-servants. And his fellow-servants were glad when
they received the food, and began to pray for him, that
he might find greater favour with his master, because he
had treated them thus. His master heard of all these
doings, and again rejoiced greatly at his conduct. The
master again assembled his friends and his son, and reported to them what he had done with the food which
he had received, and they were still more pleased that the
servant should be made joint-heir with his son."

A little later on the angel explains this passage. There
is first a confused discussion as to the work of the Son,
and it is not easy to be sure whether the reference is to
the Holy Spirit or to Jesus, but finally the following clear
statement is given: "The Holy Spirit which is pre-existent,

which created all creation, did God make to dwell in the flesh which he willed. Therefore this flesh, in which the Holy Spirit dwelled, served the Spirit well, walking in holiness and purity, and did not in any way defile the spirit. When, therefore, it had lived nobly and purely, and had laboured with the Spirit, and worked with it in every deed, behaving with power and bravery, he chose it as companion with the Holy Spirit; for the conduct of this flesh pleased him, because it was not defiled while it was bearing the Holy Spirit on earth. Therefore he took the Son [1] and the glorious angels as counsellors, that this flesh also, having served the Spirit blamelessly, should have some place of sojourn, and not seem to have lost the reward of its service. For all flesh in which the Holy Spirit has dwelt shall receive the reward if it be found undefiled and spotless. You have the explanation of this parable also."

These passages clearly represent God as having a Son who is the pre-existent Spirit. This Spirit is sent into human beings but leaves them if they are guilty of any misconduct. In the case of one man, however, who is not named but is obviously intended to be Jesus, the Spirit found complete obedience. The result was that the Father proposed to the Son, that is the Spirit, and to the counsellors, that is the angels, that this human being or flesh as Hermas calls it, should be exalted and glorified and put on an equality with the Son. This was done, and the implication of the book is that the same opportunity is offered to all others who are willing to follow their Lord. It is interesting to notice that, though it would be an abuse of language, it might be said that Hermas has a doctrine of the Trinity, but that his Trinity does not

[1] Cf. Sim. ix. 1: "For that Spirit is the Son of God," and the Latin (Vulgate) text of Sim. v. 5. 1, which adds to the explanation of the Parable the exact statement, "Now the Son is the Holy Spirit." It is uncertain whether this is the true text or merely correct explanation, but in general the Latin text is better than that of the Athos MS.,—the only Greek evidence at this point.

consist of Father, Son, and Spirit, but of Father, pre-existent Son, that is the Spirit, and adopted Son, that is Jesus. The exact details, however, of the relations subsisting between those three is a question more easily asked than answered, and the next investigator of Hermas will have to consider it very carefully. It is at present only possible to define the problem. As was said above, Hermas seems to imply that the Spirit existed from the beginning alongside of the Father, but he also implies the existence of many other good spirits opposed to the army of demons who people the world. These good spirits seem at times to be identified with angels, and the question will have some day to be discussed afresh of the relation of these spirits to the Spirit who is the Son of God and of both to the angels. Moreover, the question cannot be solved without taking into account the composition of Hermas. Closely connected with this problem is that of the identification of the Son of God with an angel who is sometimes described as "the most glorious angel" and sometimes named as Michael. Did Hermas think that the Spirit who was the Son is identical with Michael, or that Jesus became Michael, or in what way are the facts to be explained? Finally, did Hermas think that Christians became angels at their death?[1]

On what book did Hermas base his interpretation of Jesus? There is no proof that he made use of any of our existing gospels, just as it is very doubtful whether 1 Clement was acquainted with any of them.

There is, indeed, in 1 Clement one passage referring to the words of Jesus,[2] but it cannot be said that this is a

---

[1] See Appendix on pp. 104 ff.

[2] "Especially remembering the words of the Lord Jesus which he spoke when he was teaching gentleness and long-suffering. For he spoke thus: 'Be merciful, that ye may obtain mercy. Forgive, that ye may be forgiven. As ye do, so shall it be done unto you. As ye give, so shall it be given unto you. As ye judge, so shall ye be judged. As ye are kind, so shall kindness be shewn you. With what measure ye mete, it shall be measured to you.'"

quotation either from Matthew or Luke. It has points of similarity to both, but agrees completely with neither. No theory to explain the facts is convincing, for three are possible. It may be a confused reminiscence of the existing Gospels, or it may be the proof that a harmony was already in existence, or it may be drawn from a document which was used by both Matthew and Luke—in other words, the Q of the critics. Different minds will see different grades of probability in these three hypotheses. But there is no evidence to settle the question.

There is no satisfactory proof that the canonical gospels were known in the Church of Rome until the time of Justin Martyr. If, however, the question be discussed not on the basis of what gospel is quoted by Hermas or Clement, for none of them are by either, but merely on the ground of their doctrinal affinities, the gospel of Mark has the best claim to consideration. According to the other gospels Jesus was the Son of God from his birth, but, though Mark could be otherwise interpreted, the most obvious meaning of the gospel as it stands is that Jesus became Son of God at the baptism when the Spirit descended upon him. It can hardly be merely a coincidence that this gospel is actually attributed by tradition [1] to a Church which was at first adoptionist.

Sacramental adoptionist Christianity seems to be the nearest approach to a complete transformation to a mystery religion with no philosophy, which is found in the history of Christianity, but even here the basis is Jewish.

This is plain in its treatment of conduct. It had apparently accepted the sacramental remission of sins in baptism, and there is no trace in this of any allusion to original sin; the sins which are remitted had been committed by the Christian before his baptism, and there is no suggestion of any inheritance of sin. Hermas never

---

[1] There is no entirely convincing evidence in favour of this tradition. See, however, B. W. Bacon, "The Roman Origin of the Gospel of Mark," in *Harvard Theological Studies*, vii.

contemplated infant baptism. The baptized Christian started with a clean slate, but what would happen to him if he lapsed again into sin? The Epistle to the Hebrews clearly thought that he had no hope of further forgiveness, and Hermas refers very plainly, if not to the Epistle to the Hebrews itself, at least to teaching which it represents. This teaching was, of course, calculated either to maintain a high standard of conduct or else to change the definition of sin. Apparently none of the other mystery religions ever attached this importance to conduct after initiation, but human nature presented some difficulties in the enforcement of the Christian theory. It was found that the baptized frequently, if not always, lapsed into sin, and that the situation complained of by 4 Ezra was repeating itself.[1] What was the use of a system which offered men immortality, but only on conditions which no one could fulfil?

Hermas solved the problem by having recourse to another element in Jewish thought. He appealed to the possibility of repentance, and put his solution of the problem into the form of a revelation made to him by an

---

[1] "I answered then and said, This is my first and last saying, that it had been better not to have given the earth unto Adam: or else when it was given him, to have restrained him from sinning. For what profit is it for men now in this present time to live in heaviness, and after death to look for punishment? O thou Adam, what hast thou done? for though it was thou that sinned, thou art not fallen alone, but we all that come of thee. For what profit is it unto us, if there be promised us an immortal time, whereas we have done the works that bring death? And that there is promised us an everlasting hope, whereas ourselves being most wicked are made vain? And that there are laid up for us dwellings of health and safety, whereas we have lived wickedly? And that the glory of the Most High is kept to defend them which have led a wary life, whereas we have walked in the most wicked ways of all? And that there should be shewed a paradise whose fruit endureth for ever, wherein is security and medicine, since we shall not enter into it? For we have walked in unpleasant places. And that the faces of them which have used abstinence shall shine above the stars, whereas our faces shall be blacker than darkness? For while we lived and committed iniquity, we considered not that we should begin to suffer for it after death" (4 Ezra vii. 46-56).

angel—the Shepherd of the book. The revelation which
Hermas announces is that there is one repentance, but
only one, for those who sin after baptism. If repentance
is taken merely as an act of contrition this obviously does
little to solve the problem: it is not really sufficient to
cover the facts of human nature. But for Hermas repentance is much more than contrition. It consists apparently of cheerful submission to all the unpleasant
happenings of life, which are regarded as organised by
an angel, specially appointed for the purpose, in order
to adapt them to the improvement of sinners. From the
general characteristic of the parables it is clear that
Hermas did not contemplate the immediate restoration
of the penitent, or the immediate elimination of sin.
Penitence is for him an unpleasant process of education,
and I think he contemplates the probability that it is life-
long. Like all education it demands that the pupil shall
obey his teacher, and the teacher is in this case the angel
of repentance, who arranges life so as to make it educa-
tive. It is the beginning of the great Catholic system of
penance which it is so difficult to estimate at its full value
because of its corruption and exploitation in the Middle
Ages. Whether one believes in the existence of an angel
of repentance or not, the view that life with all its happenings is an education, which gradually teaches men, if
they are willing to accept it, how to cease to be sinful,
was a great lesson for the second century, and I do not
doubt that it had much to do with producing in the next
century a Church which, in spite of persecution, ultimately won the assent of the best part of the Roman world.
Though the form in which Hermas presented his teaching was mythological and crude it contained truths which
cannot be neglected.

No one can read *The Shepherd* of Hermas without
feeling that it has not been adequately discussed by modern scholarship. It is the key to the proper understanding
of Roman Christianity at the beginning of the second cen-

tury, but to use this key properly it must be subjected to a process of criticism to determine the relations of its constituent parts to one another, and to the contemporary or almost contemporary documents—1 Clement and the Epistle to the Hebrews.

Adoptionist Christianity was not destined to conquer the world, and though Roman Christianity proved to be the surviving form it had first to change much of its character in a manner which can with some degree of picturesque exaggeration be described as conquest by Ephesus.

The early development of Christianity in Ephesus is more obscure than it is in Rome; it ceased quite soon to flourish in its place of origin, but lived on elsewhere. The documents which represent the first stages of its growth are the later Pauline epistles, and the Fourth Gospel. They are inextricably involved in critical questions which have as yet received less attention than the synoptic problem.

This is especially true of the later epistles. In them, as distinct from the earlier epistles, we have a cosmical Christology which regards Christ as a pre-existent divine person who became a human being. Of that there is no doubt, nor can it be disputed that there are one or two passages in the earlier epistles which seem to pave the way for this kind of thought; but these passages are very few, and as it were wholly incidental. Thus the critical question arises whether these later epistles were written by the same person as the author of the earlier ones. The point has never been discussed fully in England, and by but a very few scholars on the Continent. The result is that it is only possible at present to say that three solutions are possible and are awaiting discussion. The first is that Paul's thought moved very rapidly in the last years of his life, and that the difference between the earlier and the later epistles only represents the development of his

thought. This is certainly a possible solution. There is
no literary objection to it which cannot adequately be
answered. The only doubt is the psychological question
whether the development implied is not so great as to be
improbable. A second possibility is that the later epistles
are not Pauline but are the work of some of Paul's followers. This is also possible, and from the nature of the
case scarcely admits of proof or of refutation. The third
possibility was suggested in 1877 by H. J. Holtzmann,
who thought that Ephesians represents the work of the
second generation, and that Colossians was a genuine
epistle interpolated by the author of Ephesians. It is
said sometimes that this is an incredibly complicated
hypothesis. Undoubtedly it is complicated, but so are
the facts, and those who regard it as incredible forget
that it is merely the application to the Pauline epistles
of exactly the same process as every one knows to have
been suffered by the epistles of Ignatius. Therefore this
theory also is perfectly possible, and ultimately, unless
the interest in critical questions dies out altogether, the
discussion of these three possibilities is certain to receive
fresh attention.[1]

The critical questions concerned with the Fourth Gospel
are better known. But whether it is later than the later
epistles of Paul, and whether it represents the result of
their influence or is a parallel line of thought is another
problem which has not yet been fully discussed: in any
case, it is cognate with them. No one knows who wrote
the Fourth Gospel. Tradition ascribes it to John the son
of Zebedee, but all critical probability is against this

---

[1] I have at present no clear opinion on the problem, except that I
am strongly disinclined to accept the rather popular view which
receives Colossians as Pauline and rejects Ephesians. Unless some
theory similar to Holtzmann's be accepted, I think that Colossians
and Ephesians stand or fall together. The popular distinction is
partly due to the fact that Protestant scholarship is more sensitive
to the un-Pauline ecclesiology of Ephesians, which it repudiates,
than to the un-Pauline Christology of Colossians, to which it
adheres.

theory. It seems tolerably clear that the Fourth Gospel was not written by an eye-witness, and that it implies not a knowledge of the historic Jesus so much as an acquaintance with the subapostolic Church. It is apparently an attempt to rewrite the story of Jesus in the interests of a "pre-existent" Christology, and of a high form of sacramental teaching.

Tradition connects both the later Pauline epistles and the Fourth Gospel with the Province of Asia, and especially with Ephesus. There is no reason for doubting this tradition, but it is strange how soon its creative spirit passed to Alexandria, a Church of which the origin is as obscure as the later history is famous.

Tantalising though many of these problems are, there is no doubt as to the main characteristics of the Christianity of Ephesus and its neighbourhood. Its Christology was the reverse of Adoptionist. It did not think of Jesus as a man who had become divine, but as a God who had become human. Moreover, an identification of this pre-existent being with the Logos of the philosopher was gradually approached in the later Epistles, and finally made in the Prologue to the Fourth Gospel.

The word Logos has an intricate and long history which has often been treated in books on the New Testament: it is quite unnecessary to repeat it at length. But it has not usually been sufficiently noted that the difficulty of the problems raised by it are mainly due to its use in different ways in different systems of thought. The popular Stoic philosophy, with its belief in a God immanent in the universe, could use Logos in the sense of the governing principle of the world, and as little less than a synonym, or, perhaps one should say, description of God. On the other hand, a transcendental theology such as Platonism, believing in a God entirely above all existence in the universe, needed a connecting link between God and the world, and could use Logos in this sense. Finally, a mediatising writer such as Cornutus could explain that the Logos was Hermes, and so triumphantly reconcile philosophy and myth, by giving a mythological meaning to a philosophic term.

All this is clear enough; but the difficulty begins when one asks in which sense the writer of the Fourth Gospel used the phrase. Did he mean that the Logos was the *anima mundi?* The phrase "the true light which lighteth every one" is susceptible of such a meaning. But it seems more probable that his theology was in the main transcendental, and that the Logos was for him the connecting link between God and the world. But how far is the Prologue really metaphysical and not comparable in its identification of Jesus and the Logos to Cornutus,[1] with his identification of Hermes and the Logos?

Further problems arise if an effort is made to reconstruct fully the Ephesian Christianity of which the Fourth Gospel is the product. After the Prologue the Logos does not seem to be mentioned again; Jesus appears as the supernatural Lord (though this word is not characteristic of the Gospel) who reveals the Father to men. He offers them salvation by regeneration in baptism, and by eating his flesh and blood in the Eucharist. They become supernaturally the children of God. This is the teaching of the Hellenised Church, not of the historic Jesus. But running through the Gospel there is also another line of thought which regards salvation as due to knowledge rather than sacraments. What is the relation to each other of these two ways of regarding salvation? The problem has scarcely been formulated by the students of the Fourth Gospel, much less adequately discussed.

Obviously the tendency of Ephesian Christianity was to minimise the human characteristics of the historic Jesus, and to merge into Docetism. This can be seen in the Fourth Gospel, and in the allied Johannine Epistles. The writer is fully aware of the danger, and protests

---

[1] Τυγχάνει δὲ Ἑρμῆς ὁ λόγος, ὃν ἀπέστειλαν πρὸς ἡμᾶς ἐξ οὐρανοῦ οἱ θεοί. Cornutus, *De Natura Deorum*, xvi.

against Docetism, but his own writings with very small changes would have been admirably adapted for Docetic purposes.[1]

If Ephesian Christianity had never come to Rome, and met its complement in the Adoptionists, it might, in spite of the Fourth Gospel, have degenerated into thorough-going Docetism, or have been represented only by Gnostics. It is hard either to prove or to refute the suggestion that Alexandrian Gnosticism of the Valentinian type came from Ephesus along the Syrian coast, and that the ultimately successful Catholicism of Pantaenus and Clement came from the other stream which passed first northwards and then through Italy to Alexandria. Each of these streams accumulated new ideas on the way: the stream passing through Syria found the Eastern Gnostics of whom Simon Magus is alleged to have been the first. The other stream passed through Rome and found Adoptionism. The combination with this strengthened the belief in the true humanity of Jesus, and in his real divinity, thus providing the groundwork for the Christological development of Irenaeus and his successors in the fourth century.[2]

The man who seems to have brought Ephesian Christianity to Rome was Justin Martyr, sometimes called the Philosopher. This title is somewhat unfair to philosophers, for the only claim which Justin could make to the name was that he had dabbled with little profit in many schools before he was converted to Christianity by an old man who gave him the Christian interpretation of the Old Testament.

Justin is in fact not much more philosophic than

[1] The Leucian Acts of John and Andrew, which seem to have a real connection with the Johannine tradition, represent this Docetic tendency.

[2] I must emphasise the speculative nature of this suggestion. So far as I know, there is not any evidence that Pantaenus was in Rome, or that Clement was influenced by Roman thought. But—merely as a guess—the idea appeals to me as probable in itself.

Hermas. His Christology is the incarnation of the Logos; but Logos is for him merely the name of a second God who is responsible for creation and redemption. Of the many books which he is said to have written only his two Apologies and his Dialogue with Trypho are extant. The latter is a long rambling exposition of the proof from the Old Testament, in the Septuagint version, that there is a "second God," and that his incarnation in Jesus was foretold. The Apologies also are full of proof from the Old Testament, but contain most valuable statements as to the Christian cult and its sacraments. They are also remarkable for insisting that the heathen religions are due to the clumsy efforts of demons to deceive men by false fulfilments of scripture.

Justin was not a man of commanding intellect, but he seems to have brought Ephesian Christianity to Rome, and so began in that city the synthesis with Greek philosophy which the later Pauline epistles and Fourth Gospel began in Ephesus and Origen completed in Alexandria. He appears to have been martyred in Rome, perhaps owing to the hostility of Crescens, a cynic philosopher with whom he had quarrelled. The acts of his martyrdom are extant; the most significant point in them is his dissociation from other bodies of Christians in Rome.[1] This is seen from the following extract from his examination by Rusticus the Prefect:

"Rusticus the prefect said, 'Where do you assemble?' Justin said, 'Where inclination and ability lead each of us. For do you really think that we all assemble in the same place? That is not the case, because the God of the Christians is not locally circumscribed, but, though he cannot be seen, fills heaven and earth and receives worship and glorification from the faithful in all places.' Rusticus the prefect said, 'Tell me where you assemble

[1] The address in Rome which Justin gives is obscure, but it is supposed to be the same as the bath called Novatian's on the Via Viminalis. See Otto's note on the subject.

or in what place you collect your disciples.' Justin said,
'I am staying above the baths of a certain Martin, the son
of Timothinus, and throughout this period (it is my second visit to Rome) I am unacquainted with any other
assembly except that in this house. And if any one wished
to come with me, I communicated to him the words of
truth.' " [1]

It would be possible to fill a volume with the discussion of the development of the Logos doctrine after the time
of Justin Martyr. All that can here be done is to note how
it passed from Rome to Alexandria—from Justin to Origen
—and to compare certain aspects of it with Adoptionist
Christianity, and to consider the position which either of
these Christologies can take in modern theology.

It is very doubtful whether Justin Martyr or the writer
of the Fourth Gospel had any concept of Immaterial
Reality. To Justin Martyr, at least, the Logos appears
to have been a second God, and his identification of Jesus
with the Logos is much more like that of Cornutus—
mutatis mutandis—than anything else which we possess.
But however this may be, the Logos Christology was invaluable for Origen in finding room in Christian theology
for the identification of God with Immaterial Reality.
We may paraphrase rather than explain his teaching by
saying that he believed in the divinity and unity of
Immaterial Reality, but thought also that diversity as
well as unity could be predicated of it; that man belonged
on one side of his nature to Immaterial Reality, and

[1] 'Ρουστικὸς ἔπαρχος εἶπε' Ποῦ συνέρχεσθε ; 'Ιουστῖνος εἶπεν' Ἔνθα ἑκάστῳ
προαίρεσις καὶ δύναμίς ἐστι. πάντως γὰρ νομίζεις ἐπὶ τὸ αὐτὸ συνέρχεσθαι
ἡμᾶς πάντας ; οὐχ οὕτως δέ· διότι ὁ θεὸς τῶν Χριστιανῶν τόπῳ οὐ περι-
γράφεται, ἀλλὰ ἀόρατος ὢν τὸν οὐρανὸν καὶ τὴν γῆν πληροῖ καὶ πανταχοῦ ὑπὸ
τῶν πιστῶν προσκυνεῖται καὶ δοξάζεται. 'Ρουστικὸς ἔπαρχος εἶπεν' Εἰπέ
ποῦ συνέρχεσθε ἢ εἰς ποῖον τόπον ἀθροίζειν τοὺς μαθητάς σου ; 'Ιουστῖνος
εἶπεν' Ἐγὼ ἐπάνω μένω τινὸς Μαρτίνου τοῦ Τιμοθίνου βαλανείου, καὶ παρά
πάντα τὸν χρόνον τοῦτον (ἐπεδήμησα δὲ τῇ 'Ρωμαίων πόλει τοῦτο δεύτερον)
καὶ οὐ γινώσκω ἄλλην τινὰ συνέλευσιν εἰ μὴ τὴν ἐκείνου. καὶ εἴ τις ἐβούλετο
ἀφικνεῖσθαι παρ' ἐμοί, ἐκοινώνουν αὐτῷ τῶν τῆς ἀληθείας λόγων.

that, so far as he did so, he shared the attribute of eternity. Like other thinkers, Origen failed to make clear exactly what is the relation between the Immaterial Reality which is eternal and changeless and the Material Reality which is subject to change and time, and is the basis of phenomena. But in some way, he believed, the Logos [1] was that power of Immaterial Reality which stretches out and mingles with the world of matter. It is impossible and undesirable to expound at length this general theory; it must suffice to notice its bearings on Christology.

In the first place, it seems to have overcome the tendency of Logos theology to produce Docetism. The earlier forms of this kind of teaching which represented the Logos as a spirit who came down to rescue humanity offered no real reason for maintaining the true humanity of Jesus. It seems to have been the pressure of recognised fact, which had not yet been forgotten, which made the writer of the Fourth Gospel and of the First Epistle of John protest so strongly against Docetism. The tendency of their teaching by itself was all the other way, and the Acts of John, with their completely unreal humanity of Jesus, are the natural, though no doubt unlooked-for, results of the Ephesian school. But that is not the case with Origen, and cannot be the case with any Christology or theology which really understands the doctrine of Immaterial Reality. It is possible to have a spirit, using the word in the popular and material sense, which looks like a human being, but is not really one, but that cannot be so with Immaterial Reality.

Origen achieved a synthesis with Greek philosophy which enabled Christianity to accept a belief in Immaterial Reality without a Docetic Christology, but it must be remembered that Origen was able to do this largely because he stood in the line of succession from the Fourth

[1] The elements of multiplicity, he thinks, are contained in the Logos, which is therefore secondary to the Father.

Gospel and Justin Martyr. He did not take the word Logos in the same sense as Justin had done, and he permanently changed, and indeed partly confused, Christian terminology by giving the meaning of immaterial to the words spirit and spiritual. They have in the main retained this meaning ever since, but students of the New Testament will do well to remember that this is not the meaning of the words in the original, and that Origen, though neither the first nor the last, is probably the ablest of the long line of theologians who have introduced metaphysics into Christian doctrine by a perverse exegesis of the words of Scripture.

The Catholic Christianity which emerged from the struggle between Adoptionism and the Logos Christology was a curious combination of both. In the strict sense of Christology, Adoptionism was completely abandoned. Jesus was regarded as the eternal Logos who became man, not as the inspired and perfect man who became God. But in the sphere of soteriology the legacy of Adoptionism can clearly be seen. The Christian became the adopted son of God, joint heir with Christ, and this remained part of Catholic teaching. It is not, however, really consistent with the Logos doctrine, and is logically part of Adoptionism. The incoherence introduced at this point was met by the splendid paradox of Irenaeus and Athanasius that God became man in order that man might become God. But splendid though this be, it remains a paradox, and it was diluted very considerably in later theology, which seems to have felt that the abandonment of Adoptionism in the sphere of Christology necessitated its abandonment in the doctrine of salvation. Thus, at least in popular theology, the grandiose conception of the apotheosis of humanity has passed into the far more mythological one of becoming an angel after death—a view very widely held, though perhaps never officially recognised.

What part can either Adoptionism or the Logos Christology play in any modern form of thought? Adoptionism seems to me to have no part or lot in any intelligent modern theology, though it is unfortunately often promulgated, especially in pulpits which are regarded as liberal. We cannot believe that at any time a human being, in consequence of his virtue, became God, which he was not before, or that any human being ever will do so. No doctrine of Christology and no doctrine of salvation which is Adoptionist in essence can come to terms with modern thought.

The doctrine of the Logos is on a different plane. In the form in which it is presented by Justin Martyr it is probably as unacceptable as Adoptionism, but in the form presented by Origen the modern mind constantly feels that the writer is struggling to express its own thoughts, and is attracted to Origen not only by the recognition of a common purpose, but by a consciousness of a common failure, for, at the end, reality transcends thought and language, and the philosophy of Alexandria was no more completely successful than is that of our world.

I have often felt in talking with younger men of the present day how closely they have approached to the position of Origen and how far they are from him in method. If I may put into my own words the form of thought which seems to animate them, it is something of this kind. They feel that the world in which we live is the expression of some great plan or purpose or pattern which is not yet complete, which shows no sign of finality, but is ever growing in complexity; which resolves itself again and again into simplicity, and then spreads out again on a yet wider scale. The plan or purpose is not a dead mechanical thing; the life which explains it is within and not without it. Men are partly the result, but partly also the instruments or even agents of this purpose. Wisdom is the right understanding of its nature; and righteousness is the attempt to subordinate human purposes to this great purpose of life. For man is not only an effect, he is a cause. When he acts, he brings into existence a new cause of which the results will follow in accordance with the established laws of reality. But there is a moment of choice, when he has it within his power to decide whether he will act or not. If he choose right, his actions will be taken up into the great web of existence, consistently with the great purpose. If he choose wrongly, the results will in the end be destroyed, not without suffering to himself and others.

To a more vivid imagination which thinks in pictures rather than in metaphysical language, life presents itself as a great web which is slowly coming from the loom, and sometimes there seems to be behind the loom the figure of the great weaver; at other times the weaving is being carried on by men and women whose weaving sometimes conforms, sometimes does not, to an infinitely complicated but symmetrical plan which, and here is the paradoxical tragedy, they can only see in the web which has been already woven; but they know that whether what they weave will remain or not depends upon its being in accord with the pattern. And then the picture changes slightly, and it seems as though the pattern begins to reveal the same features as those dimly discerned in the weaver behind the loom. And yet again the picture changes, and it is not merely the great weaver, but the men and women who are working that reappear with him to live on in the pattern emerging in the web.

That is not the same thing as the Logos Christology or doctrine of salvation as propounded by Origen, but I think that he would have understood it had he lived now. It is not the same thing as the teaching of the Kingdom of God preached by Jesus, yet I do not think that he would have condemned it, for great men understand the thoughts of lesser ones though they themselves fail to be understood. The thoughts and words of Jesus, like those

of Origen, were borrowed from his own time and race;
they belong to the first century as those of Origen belong
to the third. No historical reconstruction can make them
adequate for our generation, or even intelligible except
to those who have passed through an education in history
impossible for most. But the will of Jesus and the will
of Origen, if we can reach them through the language
and thought of their time, have no such limitations. If
I have understood them rightly, both were animated by
a desire to accomplish the purpose of God, the God who
is life.[1] And that purpose did not appeal to them as the
achievement for themselves of any salvation, in this world
or in the world to come, beyond the reach of other men,
but rather to show them what is the way of life, the natural
way, consistent with the purpose of God and the pattern
of life. So far as they succeeded in their teaching they
did so because they devoted themselves to expressing
clearly what they wished without troubling to ask whether
it conformed to what other people said, and they spoke
the clearest language which they could find in their own
generation.

To do the same thing is the business of preachers and
teachers to-day. The man who tries merely to repeat the
thoughts or the words of past generations forgets that the
call which comes to the teacher is not to repeat what others
have said because they have said it, but to say what is
true because it is true, and to say it in the language of
his own time that it may be intelligible. He will often
appear to contradict the thought or the language of Jesus
or of Paul or of Origen, but he will be loyal to the purpose
which was theirs, and yet so much more than theirs.

---

[1] Perhaps the most significant difference between Jesus and Origen
is that Origen was inclined to find the concrete expression of the
Purpose of Life in self-realisation—he was in the best sense a
Gnostic—while Jesus found it in the service of the weak, ignorant,
and sinful, rather than merely in loyal obedience to the strong,
wise, and righteous. The two are complementary, not contradictory
—but they are not identical.

APPENDIX

THE INTERPRETATION OF *THE SHEPHERD* OF HERMAS

I AM glad to be allowed to quote on this subject from a letter by my friend and former pupil, Dr. F. S. Mackenzie of Montreal, who has spent much time on the study of Hermas. He says:

"In several passages Hermas speaks of a small circle of six superior angels. It is legitimate to look for a reason for his choice of this particular number, and there can be little doubt that the reason may be discovered in Sim. ix., where the Son of God, who appears as lord of the tower, is clearly thought of as the seventh angel, superior to the six who accompany him and who have charge of the building of the tower, as they in turn are superior to all lesser angels and men. Thus the number of the archangels is made complete, according to prevailing apocalyptic enumeration. The contention of some scholars, among whom Zahn is the most outstanding, that Hermas makes a fundamental distinction between the Son of God and all angels, cannot be made good. The lord of the tower in Sim. ix. is not different in kind from the six angels who accompany him in his inspection of the tower. While he is, indeed, much more glorious than the others, nevertheless he and they alike appear as 'glorious men.' They all are angels (Sim. ix. 12. 7-8). Moreover, this angelic Son of God is called Michael in Sim. viii., and is obviously identical with the most revered or glorious angel (σεμνότατος ἄγγελος) referred to in other places. He is supreme in the angel world. He has all authority over both angels and men. He is lord of the Church, and judge of its members.

"Why is the Son of God, the Christian archangel, called Michael? Michael was one of the seven Jewish archangels; and to him, according to Dan. xii. 1, was to be committed the judgement of the people of God. There are indications in apocalyptic literature that he was regarded as supreme in this angelic circle. Hermas apparently has carried over the name of this Jewish angel, and used it to designate the archangel of the Christians, who are for him, of course, the true Israel. The position of supremacy in the angel world, assigned by pre-Christian righteous men to Michael, is really held by the Son of God. He is in fact the true Michael; and in him all that is foretold of Michael in valid prophecy will be fulfilled. If Hermas regarded the prediction of Dan. xii. 1 as authoritative at all, he must obviously have seen in it a reference to the Christian judgement to be executed by the Son of God. And I consider it highly probable that this may explain the apparent identification of the Son of God with the Jewish angel. Hermas has simply made use of the name to connect his ideas with the Danielic prophecy, and to show how, in his opinion, that prophecy is to be fulfilled. If this be so, then the Son of God is not, strictly speaking, identified with the Jewish Michael, but he may nevertheless be given the name on occasion, because of the fact that in him all that the prophets foretold of the archangel of the people of God will come to pass.

"The term Son of God is used by Hermas in a double sense. On the one hand, it is used of the pre-existent counsellor of God, who may also be called the Holy Spirit, and on the other of the glorified and exalted Jesus, the elect servant, who *became* the Son of God (Sim. v. 6), or in whom, as is said in Sim. ix. 12, the pre-existent Son became manifest. Because Jesus alone of all men preserved the indwelling Spirit pure, therefore he is the only perfect manifestation of the Spirit or Son of God. And he was rewarded for his fidelity by being adopted into the family of God as joint heir with the Son. Nevertheless he is not, and never can be, one with the pre-existent Son or Spirit.

"One is tempted to argue that this distinction is observed in Similitudes v., viii., and ix., and that the Son of the master of the vineyard, the great spreading tree, and the ancient rock respectively represent the pre-existent Son, while the elect servant, the angel Michael, and the lord of the tower represent the exalted Jesus. Thus all the angelic representations of the

Son of God would refer only to the latter. Moreover, there are features in the angelology of Hermas which strengthen such an argument. From Vis. ii. 2, 7, Sim. ix, 24. 4, 25. 2, 27. 3, it seems clear that Christians are believed to become angels at their death. Their rank, however, in the angel world will not be uniform, but will vary according to the excellence of their life on earth. Jesus therefore, because of his unique purity of life, must necessarily be the most highly exalted of all such angels. And so, in point of fact, he is. Of all angels, only he has ever been admitted to a position of co-equality with the pre-existent Son.

"On the other hand, it must be remembered that Hermas at times seems to think of the pre-existent Son or Spirit as an angel (Mand. vi. 2, xi. 9). Moreover, in his representation as the son of the master in the parable of Sim. v., he stands in very much the same relation to the first-created angels as does the lord of the tower in Sim. ix. And finally, there is an undoubted difficulty in supposing that the six archangels are thought of as being obliged to wait from the beginning of time until the exaltation of Jesus for their number to be completed. It still remains an open question whether the Christian arch-angel, the lord and judge of the Church, is the eternal or the adopted Son of God; and with the uncertainty and obscurity of the data, it may be doubted whether a final judgement in the matter can be given. Hermas does not, in fact, preserve any clear distinction between spirits and angels. He reveals throughout an undoubted fondness for hypostatisation. Even virtues and vices, emotions and passions, are described as spirits or demons as the case may be, and spoken of as if they were possessed of personality. And certainly some allowance ought to be made for this tendency of the author, in the matter of determining his conception of spirits in general, and in particular of the Holy Spirit, who besides having an eternal existence with God, dwells also in every man."

ADDITIONAL NOTE TO PAGE 74

AFTER this passage was ready for the press my friend, Mr. Robert P. Casey, sent me the following criticism: "It can hardly be said that 'we' gain through the loss of our personalities, since 'we' (a personal pronoun) *are* our personalities. On the other hand, it is quite conceivable that that Immaterial Purpose, which works in and through our personal life, or at least some parts of it, gains by rejecting us after our usefulness is past, seeking its further completion in those who come after us, and thus maintaining a unified and eternal Life through a multiplicity and diversity of lives. That this process is a gain from the point of view of history is apparent, yet it can hardly be said to be 'our' gain if 'we' are destroyed in the process.

"Furthermore, is the archipelago a fair analogy? In the sentence 'If those islands could have thought and spoken . . .' the fact that they cannot destroys the analogy at its most important point. The allegory fits admirably the relation of the individual life and Immaterial Reality as a whole, but the crux of the problem of immortality from the point of the individual is the relation between (1) the unity established between the intellectual and moral elements (but not many other elements, *e.g.* evil) of his personal life and the sum total of Immaterial Reality, and (2) the equally real and more obvious unity presented by his own personality, including all his conscious experiences regardless of their value.

"The first unity is, if not everlasting, at least as permanent as history itself, and is by its nature eternal and immaterial. The second unity is apparently transitory, being dependent physically on the brain and nervous system, psychically on the persistence of memory. Thus, to say a man has eternal life is simply to mean that certain of his activities or experiences have the attribute of eternal or immaterial. It, however, leaves untouched the question whether the 'ego' which is conscious of these activities continues after death."

The point seems to me to be well taken, and to express a widely spread and possibly correct opinion; yet I cannot but feel that Mr. Casey is a little too much influenced by the exigencies of language. Of course in all the ordinary dealings of life that which makes me "me" is a number of factors, which, taken together, may be called personality, but the real point at issue is whether in the last analysis these factors are part of "me," or are instruments which "I" use and circumstances under which "I" live. For myself I see no reason to doubt that most of them come to an end with death. But behind all this there seems to me to be something in "me" which is Immaterial, and therefore eternal, and I believe that it is this, not that which now makes up my personality, which really makes me "me."

108

INDEX

Abraham, 14, 40
Academics, 68
Achaea, 51
Acts of the Apostles, 28, 29, 30, 37, 47, 49, 50, 51, 65, 66
  of John, Leucian. *See* John
Adoptionism, 76, 77, 78, 79, 80, 81-83, 85, 89, 92, 94, 96, 98, 100-101
Age to Come, 15-16, 17, 19-21, 37, 38, 52, 58
Akiba, 12, 13
Allen, W. C., 42
Alexandria, 94, 96, 97, 98, 101
Alexandrians, 44
Ambrose, 7
Ammonius Saccus, 67
Animism, 2
Antioch, 30, 44-56, 78
  missionaries from, 65
Antiochus Epiphanes, 5
Apocalypses, 11, 38, 39
Apostles' Creed, 71
Apotheosis, 6, 100
Apuleius, 3, 63
Aquinas, St. Thomas, 8-9
Aristotle, 8, 68
Asia, 51, 94
Asians, 44
Astronomy, 8
Athanasius, 100
Augustine, 76

Bacon, B. W., 89
Baptism, 64-66, 67, 76, 89, 90, 95
Barnabas, 47, 48, 50
Bartimaeus, 37
Box, G. H., 15
Burkitt, F. C., 49, 64

Caesar, cult of, 4, 5
Caesarea, 47

Caligula, 5
Canon, Christian, 55
Censors, mediaeval, 12
Charles, R. H., 11
Christ. *See* Jesus
Christ, pre-existent, 81
Christians, Greek, 64
  Hellenistic, 62
  Jewish, 75
Christianity, Adoptionist. *See* Adoptionism
  Bible, 55
  Catholic, 60, 61, 100
  Ephesian, 95-97
  Hellenistic, 47
  Jewish, 29-30
  Roman, 91, 92
  Sabellian, 63
  Sacramental, 76
Christology, 42, 69, 85, 92, 99, 100
  Docetic, 99
  Logos, 100, 101, 102
  pre-existent, 77-78, 79-83, 94
Church, the, 31, 70, 84, 85, 107
Cilicians, 44, 45
Clemen, C., 49
Clement, 7, 96
  Epistle of, 80, 83-85, 88, 89, 92
Colossians, Epistle to the, 93
Constantinople, 10
Conybeare, F. C., 77
Corinth, 30, 53, 56-74, 79, 80
Corinthians, First Epistle to, 68, 69
  Epistles to, 48, 75
Cornelius, 45, 46, 66
Cornutus, 94, 95, 98
Councils, local, 5
Creation, 64
Crescens, 97
Cross, 61

109